Northwest Oregon

Philip N. Jones

THE MOUNTAINEERS • SEATTLE

THE MOUNTAINEERS: Organized 1906
"...to explore and study the mountains, forests,
and watercourses of the Northwest."

First edition: first printing February 1982,
second printing August 1983, third printing July 1985

Published by The Mountaineers
306 2nd Ave. W., Seattle, Washington 98119

Published simultaneously in Canada by Douglas & McIntyre, Ltd.
1615 Venables Street, Vancouver, British Columbia V5L 2H1

Maps and photos by the author
Book design by Elizabeth Watson
Cover design by Marge Mueller

Cover photo: Upstream end of the Youngs River, Trip 38
Title photo: Kayaks on Long Island, Trip 40

Manufactured in the United States of America

Library of Congress Cataloging in Publication Data

Jones, Philip N.
    Canoe routes.

    Bibliography: p.
    Includes index.
    1. Canoes and canoeing—Oregon—Guide-books.
2. Oregon—Description and travel—1951-
Guide-books.   I. Title.
GV776.07J66   1982   917.95   81-18860
ISBN 0-89886-043-1   AACR2

TABLE OF CONTENTS

INTRODUCTION

WILLAMETTE RIVER

TRIBUTARIES OF THE WILLAMETTE RIVER

COLUMBIA RIVER

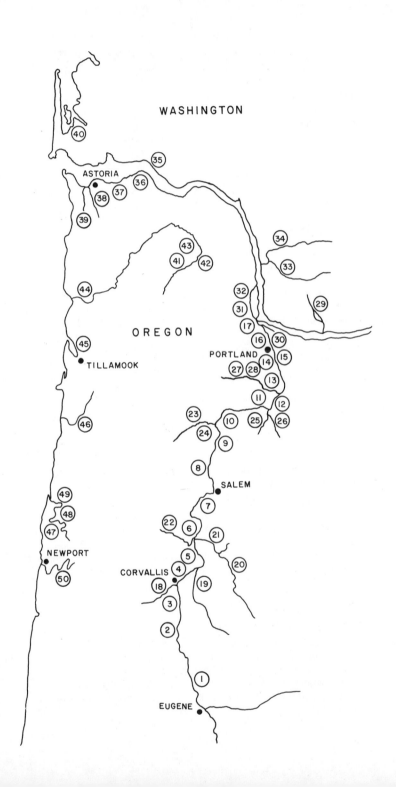

THE COAST

Searching for deep water in Tillamook Bay

ACKNOWLEDGMENTS

The author would like to credit the assistance of many people, in addition to the patient help provided by the editor, Molly M. Killingsworth, and the staff at The Mountaineers. Ed Newville offered advice and encouragement and helped paddle several of the trips. Jack Holmgren reviewed portions of the manuscript and accompanied the author on more than a dozen trips, several of which were to locations sufficiently unpleasant as to warrant exclusion from the book. Steve Moore also reviewed portions of the manuscript and made many helpful suggestions and corrections. David Puls gave tips on mapmaking and spent countless winter and spring days paddling through rain, cold, and dark of night with the author. The book would have been considerably more difficult to complete without his skillful paddling and consistent help. Special appreciation must be expressed to Holly Mitchell, who helped paddle more trips than she can remember, reviewed and typed the manuscript, and spent hours double-checking the names and locations of obscure roads and parks. Any remaining errors are solely the fault of the author, who would appreciate their being called to his attention.

INTRODUCTION

The rivers and bays of western Oregon were once the centers of civilization for the area. To the first inhabitants, the Indians, the waters offered both food and transportation. To the white man, who domesticated animals and cultivated the soil, the rivers were used primarily as economical highways, first by flatboats and bateaus, later by steamboats, and still later by tugs and barges. Today, although several of the ports of the lower Willamette and Columbia continue to rely on the rivers for commerce, most of the smaller communities have all but forgotten the rivers and the role they played in the growth of the region.

These waters now remain largely in the same condition in which the Indians and pioneers saw them. While farmland is being destroyed by freeways and subdivisions, the rivers have been nearly ignored by progress. As a result, they offer secluded canoeing in near-wilderness settings.

This guide is an attempt to catalog some of the flatwater canoeing opportunities in northwestern Oregon; a few trips spill over into southwestern Washington. The area covered is roughly the Willamette Valley from Eugene north to Portland, the lower Columbia River and its tributaries, and the coast from the Yaquina River north to Willapa Bay.

All of the included trips can easily be paddled in one day or less. The Willamette River, for example, has been divided into 17 trips of a few hours each, although the trips can be combined into tours lasting several days.

None of the included trips could be classified as whitewater, except perhaps during times of unusual flooding. Most are suitable for novice paddlers equipped with an open canoe and some common sense, but a few are on fairly swift streams that require paddling skills not possessed by a beginner; read the trip descriptions carefully when selecting a trip.

THE TRIP DESCRIPTIONS

For each of the 50 trips described in this book, the following information is summarized in capsule form at the beginning of the description:

Location: A general indication of the area in which the trip is located is given, usually by reference to a nearby city or town.

Distance: For most of the trips, an estimate of the distance to be covered is given in miles. For river trips, the mileage should be quite accurate, since it is based on the river miles shown on U.S. Geological Survey topographic maps. In some cases, however, the distances to be covered may be estimated due to recent changes in riverbeds (e.g., the Pudding River). Only a distance range, such as "from 2 to 6 miles," is given for trips on lakes or bays, since no specific route is described.

Time: The estimate of time is to be regarded as a rough guess of how much time will be spent on the water, since the type of boat, ability of the paddlers, and water level all affect speed. These estimates are on the generous side and allow enough time for a leisurely pace, but do not include driving time or time spent shuttling cars. After paddling a few of these trips, the reader will be able to adjust the author's estimates based on individual experience.

Maps and Charts: The U.S. Geological Survey (USGS) topographic maps and the National Oceanographic and Atmospheric Administration (NOAA) charts for each trip are indicated. The former are available for all of the trips described here, although in some instances four or five sheets are necessary for complete coverage of a particular trip. References are made to either the 7.5 minute series (7.5') or the 15 minute series (15') of USGS maps. The NOAA charts, however, are available only for the coast, the Columbia, and the Willamette north of Newberg. Thus, for trips on coastal rivers, portions of the Willamette, or tributaries of the Columbia or Willamette, either no chart is listed, or the indicated chart covers only a portion of the trip. A more detailed discussion of available maps occurs later in this introduction.

Best Season: The majority of the trips described in this book are canoeable all year. Trips on the coast, the Columbia, and the main channel of the Willamette are included in this category. Some of the trips, however, are not navigable year-round due to seasonal fluctuations of water levels. Included in this category are some of the smaller rivers and backwater sloughs. "Best Season" is an indication of when the water level on a particular stream will usually be high enough to allow canoeing. This indication may be of little value during periods of unusually heavy rainfall, severe drought, or when water is being released from upstream reservoirs. "Best Season" is also not an indication of when each trip is at its best for other purposes, such as wildlife observation. In most cases, the text of each trip will point out the best times for such opportunities.

Rating: Each trip is rated for difficulty according to the following rating system that is in widespread use:

Class	Characteristics
A	Still water or rivers with less than a 2 m.p.h. current; suitable for novices.
B	Rivers with a current between 2 and 4 m.p.h.; some maneuvering skill required.
C	Rivers with a velocity above 4 m.p.h., or with rapids or turns that require significant maneuvering skill.

The use of a rating system has many advantages, the principal one being that it brings a degree of standardization to describing difficulties that might be encountered on a particular river. However, no rating system can be completely accurate or free from subjective considerations.

When using this book, the ratings should be viewed as a general description of the type of water to be encountered and the speed of the water in particular, but the ratings should not be relied upon exclusively. For example, an A rating has been assigned to several trips located near the mouth of the Columbia River, since the current will usually be fairly slow, but on stormy days these particular trips can be very dangerous. The reader should examine the entire trip description and take into account the effects of weather, flooding, tides, low water conditions, and other hazards, some of which are discussed elsewhere in this introduction.

In some cases, the trips described in this book involve short portages around rapids, waterfalls, dams, or small logjams. These obstacles are mentioned within each trip description and are not taken into account in the ratings, since it is assumed that the reader will not attempt to paddle through them. Once again the assigned rating, by itself, would mislead the reader.

CHOICE OF CRAFT

A flatwater paddler has two basic choices of boats to use: a canoe or kayak. Each in turn comes in a variety of sizes and shapes to suit every intended use.

Often the two types of boats seem to merge, as in a fiberglass decked canoe or a large open touring kayak. Two basic differences remain, however. First, the canoe paddler sits at the level of the gunwales, or sometimes kneels. The kayaker, on the other hand, sits low in the boat with legs outstretched. Second, the canoeist uses a relatively short single-bladed paddle while the kayak paddler uses a longer paddle with blades at each end.

Canoes

Canoes come in a variety of lengths, the most common being 16 to 19 feet. The shorter boats, while highly maneuverable and easy to carry, have a smaller capacity and are frequently unsuitable in rough water due to a low freeboard (the distance between gunwales and waterline). Larger boats are heavier and somewhat less maneuverable, but have greater capacity and (due to their longer waterlines) are generally faster to paddle.

The shape of the hull can radically alter the above characteristics. A deep boat (said to have a high "freeboard") deflects waves and increases the volume of cargo the boat can carry, but has the disadvantage of catching the wind when the paddler would just as soon it would not. A high bow or stern has similar trade-offs: waves are less likely to spill into the boat, but a cross wind is difficult to deal with.

The keel (or lack of one) is critical. A smooth-bottomed boat turns easily, but tracks (travels in a straight line) poorly. The rocker has a similar effect: a boat with a flat bottom is stable and holds its course well, but will not turn as easily as one with a keel line whose ends are upturned similar to a rocker on a rocking chair. Boats specifically designed for flat water have little or no rocker, but have a thin keel running the length of the boat. Whitewater boats usually have a slight rocker but no keel. Some paddlers consider a small "shoe keel" to be a good compromise.

Construction materials are as varied as hull designs. Chronologically, the first canoes in the Pacific Northwest were dugout logs, while Indians in other parts of North America were using bark or animal skin boats. A handful of craftsmen still make birch bark canoes for the purist trade. Canvas-covered wood boats came next and are still widely available. They are beautiful if properly maintained, but are rather expensive.

Next came the two modern materials that have become the most popular: fiberglass and aluminum. Each has its advantages and its staunch advocates. Aluminum has long been considered the more durable of the two, and thus many whitewater paddlers favor it. A disadvantage, however, is that

Flatwater boats: Top, *one-person slalom kayak;* center, *a seventeen-foot aluminum canoe, paddled solo;* bottom, *a two-person inflatable kayak.*

*Touring kayaks—designed for rough saltwater—can also be used on flat freshwater.
Top, a German-made folding Klepper, equipped with sails and leeboards; bottom, a
two-person Klepper, paddled solo.*

aluminum is difficult to repair. Fiberglass, on the other hand, while somewhat less durable, can be repaired relatively easily at home or in the field. Fiberglass is available in a wider selection of hull designs suitable for flat water, white water, or racing. Fiberglass is also quieter than aluminum as it moves through rough water.

These generalizations must be considered in light of the fact that manufacturing techniques used for both aluminum and fiberglass vary to suit particular needs. Aluminum boats can vary in the type of aluminum used, the gauge of the sheet metal, the riveting technique, and the number of reinforcing ribs. Fiberglass hulls range widely in weight, primarily due to the construction techniques and type of plastic used. Superlight fabrics, previously used only on competition whitewater kayaks, are now being applied to recreational canoes.

Newer materials are also appearing on the market to compete with aluminum and fiberglass. One of the most successful involves a plastic and foam sandwich. Marketed under several trade names, it is extremely durable due to its puncture resistance and its "memory" (ability to return to its original shape after deformation).

If nothing else, the novice must have realized from the above discussion that every canoe is a compromise: maneuverability versus tracking; weight versus durability and size; seaworthiness versus speed; and finally price versus quality. From reading sales literature, one would think that every manufacturer has solved the age-old trade-offs. Brochures describe every boat as tracking like an arrow while capable of turning on a dime, light as a feather but capable of rough whitewater use. Don't believe them. Be grateful if you find a manufacturer or dealer who is honest about his or her boats, enabling you to choose one that meets your particular needs and intended uses. If you're not sure what you want, rent or borrow a few to see what they're like, or seek out more experienced paddlers for advice on particular models.

Kayaks

Although canoes are the most popular craft for flatwater paddling, many paddlers prefer to use a kayak. To most people, the word *kayak* is synonymous with white water, but several models of flatwater touring kayaks are available.

A primary advantage of a flatwater kayak is that it is simply easier to paddle than a canoe, at least for novices. Even on flat water, paddling a canoe in a straight line requires no small amount of skill. When equipped with a rudder, a flatwater kayak can be paddled reasonably well by a novice after a training period of about three strokes. Well, maybe five. A kayak is also more suitable in rough water than a canoe.

Kayaks have disadvantages, too. Although flatwater kayaks can carry food and gear for two- to three-week trips, very careful packing is required; while with a canoe, bulky items needn't be left at home. And families will have a hard time squeezing children into a kayak as extra passengers.

Flatwater kayaks are available as both one-person models and those designed for two. The latter are equipped either with a single large cockpit or two smaller ones. One-person whitewater kayaks should not be ruled out for

Assembling a folding kayak

flatwater use, but the beginner should be aware of their limitations. They are very tippy and difficult to paddle in a straight line. They are, however, very maneuverable.

The flatwater kayaks are longer, higher, and wider than their whitewater counterparts, in order to accommodate cargo carried on overnight or multi-day tours. Designed to track rather than turn quickly, they are often equipped with a rudder at the rear, either fixed or operated by foot pedals.

The most incredible of these boats are the folding kayaks. Using collapsible wooden frames and fabric hulls, these boats are desirable when storage space is at a premium, or, more important, when access to wilderness water is only by light aircraft. These folding boats are considered *de rigueur* for flying into remote country. The nature of these boats and their cost generally preclude use on white water or other situations where their hulls or frames may be damaged.

Inflatable kayaks are also available, but they have limited appeal to the flatwater paddler. While compact, lightweight, and relatively inexpensive, they track poorly and move slowly. Storage space for gear is limited or nonexistent. For the serious paddler, their use would best be restricted to whitewater trips, particularly when gear can be carried in an accompanying inflatable raft.

Some general recommendations can be made based on the above information. If you have a family or bulky equipment, a canoe may be the wisest choice. If you are reluctant to learn canoe paddling, buy a kayak, particularly one with a rudder. A folding kayak is essential if you are interested in flying into remote areas, or simply need to store it in a spare closet. In any event, shop around and make sure you are getting a quality boat, not a poorly designed toy. With proper care, it should be an investment and a pleasure for a lifetime.

CLOTHING

The seasons clearly dictate what clothing is appropriate, and what is not. On those rare occasions when bad weather is unlikely, T-shirts and shorts are fine, as long as extra dry clothing is carried for each person in the boat. If a capsize is remotely possible (and it always is), the extra clothing should be placed in waterproof containers and securely attached to the boat. A wetsuit is a good idea, when rough water may be encountered.

In summer, light cotton clothing that covers the arms and legs is invaluable for sunburn protection, but during the rest of the year the best fabrics are either wool or one of the new synthetic piles due to their ability to maintain warmth even when wet.

Paddling in rainy weather is not nearly as unpleasant as it sounds, if proper precautions are taken. The perfect rain gear has yet to be invented. Impervious fabrics keep out the rain, but keep in an equal amount of perspiration. Loose-fitting garments provide adequate ventilation, too much in fact during windy periods. The new breathable fabrics such as Gore-Tex work well, but the expense and the need to keep them clean will deter many users.

An important item of equipment to consider in rainy weather is a spray skirt. Used on either a kayak or a canoe, a spray skirt not only keeps rain off the paddler's legs, but also keeps the interior of the boat and any cargo dry. If a ready-made spray skirt is not available for your boat, a homemade version can usually be sewn out of waterproof fabric.

Footwear should be considered carefully. In warm summer weather, almost anything will work. Old tennis shoes, worn without socks, are good, particularly on shallow waters where frequent exits are required. In cool wet weather, such as spring and fall, waterproof boots or wetsuit booties are a good investment. Rubber-bottomed boots with leather uppers are a popular choice, but insulated models must be used on cold trips.

A hat is important in all seasons, to fend off sun in summer and rain in the other 11 months of a Pacific Northwest year. A wool brimmed hat does both, but a stocking cap is warmer.

Gloves are essential in cold weather. Wool gloves worn under waterproofed leather mittens should be considered as a minimum. In warm weather, bicycle gloves help avoid blisters while maintaining ventilation.

Sunglasses should be carried year-round to protect against not only direct sunlight, but also the glare off the water's surface.

BASIC PADDLING TECHNIQUES

A comprehensive discussion of paddling techniques is beyond the scope of this book, and probably beyond the ability of the author, but what follows is an introduction to the basic strokes used in flatwater paddling. The beginner should be warned, however, that a reading of the following few paragraphs will not qualify one to safely paddle all of the trips listed in this book. While most of the trips described here are suitable for the inexperienced, several of the trips, as noted in the trip descriptions, require a skill level that can only be acquired by on-the-water practice, preferably with the help of a more experienced paddler. What follows, then, is more of a warning of some of the complexities than a full discussion of them.

Canoe Paddling

A two-person canoe is propelled using two single-bladed paddles, usually on opposite sides of the boat. The stern paddler, who has greater available leverage, performs the primary steering of the boat. Much of the time, the bow paddler provides propulsion only.

Having considerably more influence on the direction the boat travels, the stern paddler must use the paddle to counteract the effect of paddling on one side of the boat. The principal stroke for this purpose is the J stroke: when nearing the end of the stroke, the paddler rotates the paddle slightly and strokes away from the boat for a few inches. When paddling on the left side of the boat, the path of the paddle forms a J in the water. The relative strengths of the paddlers will determine whether the J strokes made by the stern paddler will be slight or exaggerated. The stern paddler can make turns in either direction without changing sides by using either stronger or more pronounced J strokes, or the draw stroke discussed below.

For quick turns, the bow paddler should paddle on the opposite side of the boat from the direction to be turned, using a "sweep" stroke that begins close to the bow and travels in an arc away from the bow, and ending with the paddle perpendicular to the canoe. Meanwhile, the stern paddler will be J stroking on the opposite side.

Another turning technique, or to move the canoe sideways, involves paddling at right angles to the keel line of the boat. When paddling toward the boat, the stroke is called a draw; when paddling away from the boat, it is a pry. When two paddlers both pry or draw on the same side of the boat, the boat will move sideways, a useful technique for avoiding a midstream obstacle or when approaching a dock or shore. When one paddler pries and the other draws on the same side (or pries on the opposite side) the boat will rotate on its center, useful for turning in constricted places.

All of the strokes discussed above can be performed reasonably well while sitting upright on the seat of a canoe. However, many situations will require the paddler to kneel, with the knees braced against the hull and the buttocks placed against the front edge of the seat or a thwart (a brace running across the top of the canoe). In rough water, or when making a sharp turn, the added stability from kneeling is essential. Kneeling also reduces the surface area to be affected in windy weather.

Kayak Paddling

Whether a one- or two-person boat, a kayak is propelled with one or two pair of long double-bladed paddles. The overall length of the paddles depends on the type of paddling done. For flat water, a relatively long (up to eight feet) paddle is preferred, especially in a two-person boat, while a shorter one is used for white water.

Most flatwater kayak paddles are detachable at the midpoint of the shaft for storage and transport. The same connection is also used to adjust the angle between the two blades. While the beginner may think that the blades should be parallel, the most efficient use of the paddle involves a "feathered" paddle, where one blade is rotated 90 degrees from the other.

The primary advantage of a feathered paddle is the reduced drag or wind resistance of the airborne blade. Although it may seem unnecessarily complex, it is quite easy to learn. Most right-handed paddlers will adjust their paddles so that the left blade will face up, away from the water, when the right blade is being stroked. At the completion of the right stroke, the paddler flexes the right wrist backwards while allowing the shaft to rotate in the left hand. At this point, the left blade will be at a right angle to the water, ready to enter the water and be stroked. The right blade will be parallel to the water, facing down toward the water.

Most left-handed paddlers will do the opposite, using their left hand to rotate the blades and allowing the shaft to rotate in their right hand.

Once the feathered paddle is mastered, the next two most common mistakes are closely related: paddling too deeply and at too steep an angle. The end of the paddle in the water should not be submerged beyond the point where the blade meets the shaft, and the shaft should be held at a relatively shallow angle.

In a two-person boat, the stern and bow paddlers should coordinate strokes to avoid striking paddles together.

If your kayak is equipped with a foot-operated rudder, and you plan to visit only the quietest of flat water, you may skip the next few paragraphs; but if you ever venture out on fast-moving streams (of which several are described in this book), you will discover that a rudder is no substitute for knowledge of a few basic strokes. In fact, a rudder can be a liability in fast current, since it inhibits backpaddling.

Several techniques are available for turning a kayak. The simplest is called the stern rudder: the rear paddler simply places one end of the paddle in the water and holds it against the force of the moving kayak. The kayak will react by turning toward the side on which the rudder was made. Obviously, this technique works only when the boat is moving faster than the water in which it is floating.

The stern rudder produces a relatively abrupt change in course. More subtle adjustments can be made by continuing to paddle as normal, but making more forceful strokes on one side than the other.

Another technique involves paddling on one side of the boat only, perhaps combined with your partner backpaddling on the other side, but close coordination between the paddlers will be necessary. If these strokes are made in wide arcs rather than parallel to the hull, they become highly effective sweep strokes similar to the sweep strokes used in a canoe.

Kayak paddles can also be used for other purposes besides forward momentum. Sideways travel can be accomplished by draw strokes as described above for a canoe. Backpaddling is another important stroking method, particularly on swift waters when "ferrying" from one side of the channel to the other, but these are primarily whitewater techniques and are beyond the scope of this brief discussion.

Capsizes can be prevented by using the paddle in an outrigger position. Place the face of the paddle on the surface of the water in the direction which the capsize may occur. If the paddle is held firmly (or slapped forcefully), the resistance of the water against the blade will prevent a capsize (or arrest one in progress).

SAFETY EQUIPMENT

Carrying life jackets is required by law. They should be worn, not sat on or stowed in the bottom of the boat to be lost in a capsize. Since prices, sizes, styles, and comfort vary considerably, shop around. Seat cushions are available that are also legal flotation devices, but since they cannot be worn while paddling, they should not be relied upon exclusively.

An extra paddle should be tied to the boat, but not so securely as to delay its use in an emergency. Grab loops or painters should be installed at the bow and stern, and a bailing scoop should always be handy. An inexpensive scoop can be made from a large plastic container such as a bleach or milk bottle: cut off the bottom at an angle, but leave the cap on; tie the scoop to the boat with string to prevent it from being lost in a capsize.

Also, the boat itself should be equipped with flotation devices (if not built-in) for the safety of crew, cargo, and boat.

A map of some kind, either the sketch map from this book, a USGS topographic map, or a NOAA chart should always be carried, along with a compass. For those with limited experience in the use of a map and compass, several good references are available, including *Be Expert with Map and Compass* by Bjorn Kjellstrom (Scribner, 1976).

In a survival situation, such as a capsize in cold weather, several small items of equipment can make a big difference. A flashlight, first-aid kit, matches, and a chemical firestarter should be carried on every trip, and always in waterproof containers. A pocketknife should also be considered an essential.

Two other items are not essential on short flatwater trips, but should be carried on trips of any length or where a strong current will be encountered. The first is a length of rope, which is useful for lining boats through rough or shallow areas, and for rescuing people or swamped boats. A pulley will extend its usefulness. The second is a boat repair kit, for use in event of damage by rocks or other obstructions. The contents of the kit will depend, of course, on the type of boat being used. Some paddlers try to get by with just a roll of silver heating duct tape, but a more extensive kit should be considered.

SAFETY TECHNIQUES

Flatwater canoeing is a relatively safe activity if approached in an intelligent manner with a reasonable amount of caution. Even so, every year several people in Oregon manage to drown themselves, often in placid waters and only a few feet from shore.

Compliance with a few simple rules would prevent most or all of these accidents. First, a life jacket should be worn. Modern life jackets provide insulation in cool weather and are quite comfortable; any slight inconvenience is more than compensated for by the margin of safety provided. You should also remember not to wear any heavy or bulky objects such as hip boots or backpacks that might add to your weight or detract from your swimming ability.

Equally important is a realistic appraisal of your own skills as a paddler and as a swimmer. When planning a trip, gather as much information as possible about the length of the trip and the type of paddling involved, and if you have any doubts about whether your skills are evenly matched with the trip, look for an easier one or perhaps seek more skilled companions. While most of the trips described in this book are suitable for beginners, a few are not. When selecting a trip, read the entire description prior to launching, and be aware of unusual conditions (such as flood stages) that may turn calm waters into turbulent ones.

Weather is another important factor that can create dangerous conditions. Do not attempt to cross large open areas if bad weather is likely to arrive, and always carry enough rain gear and warm clothing to allow you to function when it does. If in doubt, stay close to shore rather than crossing open lakes and bays. Close to shore is also the best place to be in the event of a capsize.

If you do tip over, here are some safety suggestions:

Most boats are equipped with built-in flotation, so you should not instinctively abandon your craft. First, determine whether you are in any personal danger from downstream logs or rocks. If you are being carried downstream, try to float feet first, to cushion any impact. If possible, stay upstream from your boat. A boat loaded with gear and filled with water weighs a couple of tons and could easily crush a paddler against a log or a rock.

If you are in no immediate personal danger, determine the status of your companions, and help them as much as possible. Only then should you worry about your swamped boat or the paddle that just disappeared around the next bend. Your life, and that of your fellow paddler, is much more valuable than any boat or equipment.

If swimming to shore presents any problems due to distance, temperature, poor swimming skills, or lack of a life jacket, stay with the boat, except perhaps in swift water. You cannot control the path of a swamped boat being carried rapidly downstream, but on calm waters you may be able to remove much of the water by bailing or other techniques, which should be practiced in advance. At this point you will appreciate the fact that you have previously attached your gear to the boat in a manner that kept it inside the hull of the boat, rather than dangling it over the side. If the water is cold, remember that a swamped boat will usually float close to the surface of the water, allowing the paddlers to sit in it (or on it) and stay out of the water to a large extent.

But the most important thing to do is probably the hardest to remember: do not panic. Common sense is your best friend.

In the event serious misfortune does strike, you will want someone to come looking for you and your companions. In order for this to happen, a responsible friend should be told exactly where you are going, where you plan to leave your car, and when you plan to return.

TRANSPORTING BOATS AND SHUTTLING CARS

Canoes and kayaks are awkward items to carry on a car. Numerous roof racks are on the market; their suitability depends on both the type of boat and car involved. If your car has sizable rain gutters, easily attachable canoe racks such as the "Quick and Easy" brand are available locally or from various mail-order houses.

For kayaks as well as canoes, the Quick and Easy brackets are available separately. Combined with 2 × 4 crossbars, some old carpet scraps, and some ingenuity, an extremely strong set of racks can be made quite cheaply.

When putting a boat on a rack, make certain that the boat is securely attached to the car, not just to the rack. Freeway speeds and sudden stops can be disastrous for a poorly attached boat. On long trips, the straps should be checked frequently.

Since most of the paddle routes described here are one-way river trips, another transportation problem occurs: how to get back to the launching point, where your car is waiting. With large groups of paddlers, extra cars and drivers are usually abundant, and shuttles are easily accomplished, especially when some of the cars are capable of carrying more than one boat.

Leaving a bicycle at Paradise Point State Park for the trip back to the car.

But for a pair of paddlers, the solution to the car shuttle question is often the use of two cars and a lot of needless miles driven and gasoline consumed, particularly when only one of the cars is equipped with a roof rack.

On long trips, a third person who shuttles the cars but does not paddle is tremendously helpful, but friends like that are hard to find. Hitchhiking sometimes works, especially if you meet up with other paddlers, but hitchhiking in remote rural areas is often disappointing, if not dangerous.

On short trips, a bicycle is an excellent solution. The bike (preferably an old and rusty one) is left at the destination, either carefully hidden in the brush or securely locked, or both. At the conclusion of the trip, one of the paddlers then pedals the bike back to retrieve the car. Since the rider does not need to carry the lock while pedaling the bicycle back to the car, an entire arsenal of heavy locks and chains can be used to make sure the bike stays put.

While most paddlers do not relish the thought of a tiring bicycle ride at the end of the day, they can usually cover 10 miles or so of flat terrain in less than an hour. And besides, with luck the same person will not have to pedal after every trip! The appropriate way to begin the bike ride is with the flip of a coin to determine which paddler has the privilege of pedaling back to the car.

One other tip may make your canoe trip and car shuttle more enjoyable. Do not leave anything of value in your car while paddling, particularly if the car is left at a remote rural location. If enough people follow this simple rule, perhaps someday thieves will get tired of breaking into cars only to find an empty interior. Leave most valuables at home, and carry the few you bring along in the boat, since a wet wallet or billfold is better than none at all.

MAPS AND CHARTS

The sketch maps included in this book should be adequate for most users. They have been drawn to scale, usually 1 or 0.5 inches to the mile, although the width of rivers has often been exaggerated for clarity. For those wishing more detailed maps, each trip description includes references to U.S. Geological Survey (USGS) topographic maps and (where applicable) National Oceanographic and Atmospheric Administration (NOAA) charts.

The river miles marked on the sketch maps, the USGS maps, and the NOAA charts can be confusing. The mile distances are measured from the mouth of each stream. For example, the point where the Luckiamute River joins the Willamette River is mile 0 of the Luckiamute. The same point, measured from the mouth of the Willamette, is that river's mile 108.

USGS topographic maps are the most detailed land maps available. They are printed in several scales, but the most useful are the 7.5 and the 15 minute series. The former are more detailed than the latter and have been updated more recently. Most the the 7.5 minute series maps have been revised since the late 1960's, while the 15 minute series maps are often 20 to 30 years old. Needless to say, numerous changes in river channels and roads can occur in 30 years. The maps are available from most outdoor stores or through the mail from USGS, Box 25286 Federal Center, Denver, Colorado 80225. Free order forms and indexes are available for each state.

Key to map terms and symbols in this book

NOAA charts provide extremely detailed data on water features such as depths, bridges, powerlines, obstructions, and shorelines, but are only available for major navigable waters. In Oregon, the charts are available for the Willamette north of Newberg, the Columbia, and the coast. The charts are available at nautical supply houses, or by mail from the Distribution Division, National Ocean Survey, Riverdale, Maryland 20840. An index to Pacific Coast charts is available free of charge.

A third source of information is the series of county maps published by the Oregon and Washington Departments of Transportation. Their General Highway Series maps show rivers in reasonable detail and also show backroads not shown on gas station maps or some of the older topographic maps. Their "half size" series is especially handy. A free index and order forms are available from the Oregon Department of Transportation, Map Distribution Unit, Room 17, Transportation Building, Salem, Oregon 97310, or from the Washington Department of Transportation, Public Transportation and Planning, Highway Administration Building, Olympia, Washington 98504.

Another good source of information is the Oregon State Marine Board. In addition to pamphlets on boating safety, the board publishes a map entitled *A Guide to Oregon Boating Facilities.* The map shows the location of every public boat ramp in the state, plus the location of commercial boating marinas and moorages. Facilities located at each site are described as well. Free copies of the publication are available from the Oregon State Marine Board, 3000 Market St. N.E., Salem, Oregon 97310.

CANOEING ON THE WILLAMETTE RIVER

Seventeen of the canoe trips described in this book cover the Willamette River from south to north, from the Eugene area to Kelley Point, where the Willamette joins the Columbia north of Portland.

The trips are presented as short segments, each of which can be paddled in a day or less. Most involve only about five hours of paddling. Although paddling time and time spent driving and shuttling cars, making side trips, birdwatching, etc., usually consume the bulk of a day for most

A public dock in Nehalem

Willamette rivermile marker

river travelers, some ambitious paddlers will be able to paddle two or more adjacent trips in a single day. The trips in the Eugene-Corvallis area cover up to 20 river miles, but due to the slow current downstream, the mileage of each of the trips decreases dramatically as the river approaches sea level at Oregon City.

Public land along the Willamette can be divided into two types. The first includes boat ramps and public parks which are accessible by automobile. Each of the trips described here begins and ends at such a park or boat ramp. The second group consists of public land acquired as part of the Willamette Greenway project. These areas are not accessible by car, but for that reason, make excellent lunch spots or campsites.

Some of the greenway access areas are equipped with picnic tables, outhouses, and, occasionally, fireplaces, while others are completely undeveloped. Drinking water is rare and should either be carried from home or found in some of the towns or parks on the way.

The State of Oregon has published an excellent map of the Willamette which shows the facilities available at each park and access area. The map, called the *Willamette River Recreation Guide*, is updated from time to time, thus showing the current status of the greenway acquisition program. For a copy, write to the State Parks and Recreation Branch, Department of Transportation, Salem, Oregon 97310.

The greenway program also provided for posting the banks of the Willamette with occasional river mile markers (see photo). The signs appear sporadically, usually on public access land, but rarely exactly at the mileage they purport to mark. While they are fortunately unobtrusive, binoculars are often necessary to read them from midstream.

Oregon has many areas where canoeists can enjoy trips lasting two or more days. The Willamette is an excellent example. Depending on your pace, two, three, or four of these suggested trips could be combined for a pleasant

weekend outing, or all could be combined into a strenuous five-day trip or a relaxing week-long excursion.

Overnight trips, and the equipment carried on them, should be planned carefully. Do not count on covering distances as fast, or maneuvering as easily, with a loaded boat as with an empty one. Carry extra food, extra clothing, and make sure all of it is attached to the boat and secured in waterproof containers.

Some useful equipment for overnight trips includes the following:

A large collapsible plastic water jug enables you to carry water to campsites that have none, but takes up little room when not being used. A 2.5 gallon jug should easily be adequate for two persons on an overnight trip.

In wet weather, careful thought should be given to sleeping gear. A synthetic sleeping bag is a bit bulkier and heavier than a down-filled one, but is less expensive and has the advantage of being warm even when damp.

When camping along a river, certain basic "camping manners" should be observed out of consideration for paddlers who follow and for neighboring landowners. The purpose of these manners is to leave no trace of your passing. Most are just plain common sense, but sometimes people need to be reminded of them. Here are a few suggested rules:

1. Don't litter.
2. Keep noise to a minimum.
3. Use stoves rather than building fires, but if you do build a fire, use established fireplaces whenever possible. If you must start a fire in a new location, build a fire pit, and do your best to return the ground to its natural state afterwards (after making sure the coals are well drowned). Don't build fires up against large boulders or logs.
4. Dispose of human wastes well away from the water and any possible campsites or trails.
5. Do not camp, or otherwise trespass, on any private property.
6. Camp at least 100 feet from the river.

The main channel of the Willamette is canoeable year-round, while some of the channels behind islands (for example, Lambert Slough, described in trip #9) become quite shallow after midsummer. Spring and summer are the most popular seasons for boating, while fall is perhaps the prettiest. But do not overlook winter paddling. When properly equipped (i.e., good rain gear and several layers of wool) a winter day spent on the Willamette can be very rewarding.

At three points on the Willamette, small ferries carry auto traffic across the river. These ferries, operated by the counties in which they are located, cross at Buena Vista (north of Albany), Wheatland (north of Salem), and near Canby (south of Oregon City). Parks located near or adjacent to these ferry landings are designated as starting or ending points for several trips on the Willamette and on tributaries that enter the Willamette just upstream from the crossings.

To a large extent, these ferries are holdovers from earlier times when bridges were uncommon. They remain as quaint reminders that travel once moved at a much slower pace than it does today. The Wheatland ferry, for example, has been operating since 1844, and the Buena Vista ferry made its first crossing in the early 1850's.

When planning a trip, keep in mind that the ferry operators may keep un-

Along the East Fork of the Lewis River

predictable hours. The Buena Vista ferry does not run on weekends, and the Canby ferry does not run on winter's high waters. In addition, the services they currently provide may be curtailed in the immediate future. As of this writing (mid-1981), the Wheatland ferry is now charging a toll, and the Buena Vista ferry is being threatened by county budget cuts that may seriously limit future service. When driving to or from a trip, or making a car shuttle, do not depend on using one of the ferries; but if the ferry is running, take the few extra minutes for a ride into the past.

One other caution about the ferries: when paddling across their short routes, give them a wide berth. They are not capable of maneuvering quickly, and the operator might not see your small boat before it is too late.

TIDES

Several of the trips described in this book are on tidal waters. Obviously, the coastal bays and rivers are tidal, but most people are unaware that the Columbia and the Willamette as far south as Oregon City are also influenced by ocean tides.

Two high tides and two low tides occur each day. One of the high tides is higher than the other, and one of the low tides is lower than the other low tide. The four tides are referred to as higher high water, lower high water, higher low water, and lower low water. The height of the tides is measured in feet above mean lower low water, which is referred to as zero. Thus, a lower low water of −1.5 followed by a higher high water of 7.5 produces a total fluctuation, or tidal range, of 9 feet.

Tides must be distinguished from tidal currents. High tide and low tide indicate the high and low points of the vertically rising and falling water. Tidal currents represent the horizontal movement of the water past a given point. Ebb is the seaward flow of water, and flood is the inward flow. Slack water occurs at the moment between ebb and flood when the horizontal movement of the water is zero. In theory, slack water should occur precisely at each high tide and low tide, but in practice the highs and lows rarely coincide with slack water. Both tide tables and tidal current tables are necessary to determine the exact time of slack water, maximum ebb, or maximum flood.

The National Ocean Survey publishes detailed tide tables and tidal current tables annually. They are available for purchase at most nautical supply stores. These tables are not essential, particularly in areas where the tidal influence is weak, but should be consulted on waters closer to the Pacific, such as coastal bays and the lower portions of coastal rivers, especially the Columbia.

The small tide table booklets given out by boating and fishing stores do not include data on tidal currents, such as the velocity of the currents or when they reach their maximum, nor do they indicate the times of slack water. But they are better than nothing, since the hours and height of the tides are listed.

Because of the effect of tidal currents, coastal bays and mouths of rivers can be dangerous to small boats. The danger is greatest at maximum ebb, when the ebb tide meets the resistance of the ocean. Rough water usually results, particularly in river mouths, when river flow adds to the velocity of the ebb tide. Shallow areas accentuate the problem. Even on windless days, extremely rough conditions can result. There is a moral to this story: if you must pass through an area near the mouth of a river or bay, do it only at slack tide; and the time of slack water can be determined only by consulting a tidal current table.

Launching from Long Island at low tide

CONSERVATION

People who use rivers for any purpose have a moral obligation to leave the waters in the same condition in which they found them. In fact, the river traveler should do his or her best to leave the rivers in better condition than they were found. So not only should you refrain from littering and polluting, you should pick up after those who are not quite as considerate. Don't let bottles and cans float by; pick them up and improve the scenery a little for the next person.

The conscientious boater does his part to help clean up waterways.

In the same vein, if only out of a selfish desire to preserve one's own recreation, you should join with other environmentally inclined individuals who are working to protect local rivers from pollution and destruction. Dues to local or national environmental groups are only a few dollars a year and serve the dual purpose of helping fund their activities and keeping members informed of environmental problems through magazines and newsletters. Just a few of such groups are listed below. They deserve your support and participation.

Oregon Environmental Council
    2637 S.W. Water, Portland, Oregon 97201
Lower Columbia Canoe Club
    P.O. Box 40210, Portland, Oregon 97240
The Mountaineers
    719 Pike Street, Seattle, Washington 98101
Sierra Club
    530 Bush Street, San Francisco, California 94108
Friends of the Earth
    124 Spear Street, San Francisco, California 94105
The Nature Conservancy
    1800 North Kent Street, Arlington, Virginia 22209
Northwest Rivers Defense League
    2637 S.W. Water, Portland, Oregon 97201
Oregon Wilderness Coalition
    P.O. Box 3066, Eugene, Oregon 97403
Washington Environmental Council
    107 South Main, Seattle, Washington 98104
The Izaak Walton League of America
    1800 North Kent Street, Suite 806, Arlington, Virginia 22209
Oregon Wildlife Federation
    P.O. Box 4552, Portland, Oregon 97208

Paddlers should also keep in mind that they aren't the only ones who have the right to use rivers, be it for recreation or for commerce. Although some powerboaters have a reputation for disregarding the rights and safety of small boats (primarily by ignoring their own wakes), some of the problem could be alleviated by common sense on the part of the small boat operators. Any paddler who keeps to the middle of a river channel populated by ski boats, tugs, or large ships is asking for trouble. The same holds true when encountering fishermen. Whether fishing from a boat or from the bank, they deserve to be disturbed as little as possible. Give them a wide berth, don't paddle across their lines, don't make a lot of noise or splash around unnecessarily, and they will treat you with similar respect.

PRIVATE PROPERTY

The rivers, lakes, and bays described in this book are generally considered to be publicly owned, based on a history of public use for commerce and recreation. The same rule, however, does not apply to their shores. The canoeist should assume that the banks of all fresh water are in private ownership, with the exception of public parks, boat ramps, and highway bridges.

It is unfortunate, but paddlers cannot indiscriminately select sites for launching, lunching, or lounging without regard for the rights of private property owners. The long-term solution to the problem is the acquisition of additional park land, and the disregard of private property rights by paddlers can only increase local landowners' opposition to new parks.

In this book, public parks and access areas along each route are marked on the sketch maps. All other land should be assumed to be private.

FURTHER READING

One of the best books of instruction on canoeing is *The Complete Wilderness Paddler* by James Davidson and John Rugge (Knopf, 1978). The authors use the planning and carrying out of a major canoe expedition as the backdrop for a comprehensive and entertaining discussion of equipment and techniques used on both calm and rough waters.

For those planning saltwater kayak trips, *Sea Kayaking* by John Dowd (University of Washington Press, 1981) is an excellent book on the problems presented by ocean water and weather, particularly in remote areas where outside assistance is unlikely.

Closer to home, *Boating in Coastal Waters* (Oregon Marine Board, 1968), although somewhat dated due to recent changes in jetties, discusses the precautions necessary for safe boating in specific bays and river mouths on Oregon's coast. In the Eugene area, the city Parks and Recreation Department has printed a pamphlet entitled *Guide to Flatwater Canoeing and Camping*, devoted primarily to lakes in the Cascades and Coast Range near Eugene.

Paddlers looking for whitewater opportunities on Oregon's rivers should consult John Garren's *Oregon River Tours* (Touchstone Press, 1976) or *The Soggy Sneakers Guide to Oregon Rivers*, published in 1980 by the Willamette Kayak and Canoe Club, a Corvallis group.

For those interested in the historic aspects of Oregon rivers and river commerce, several sources are available at public libraries and local historical societies. *Willamette Landings*, by Howard McKinley Corning

Raccoon tracks on the banks of Marys River

Cloverdale

(Oregon Historical Society, 1973), gives an excellent history of the Willamette River and its early towns.

Wildlife is abundantly evident on the shores of Oregon's rivers. Several comprehensive field guides are available, but the casual observer may be better off with smaller localized handbooks. The most commonly seen birds are described in *Familiar Birds of the Northwest*, published in 1981 by the Portland Audubon Society. The same group also publishes a monthly newsletter, *The Warbler*, which discusses current birding opportunities, while up-to-the-minute reports are available by calling their "bird alert" in Portland at (503) 292-0661. When animal or bird tracks are found on muddy banks, a good reference is *Animal Tracks of the Pacific Northwest* (The Mountaineers, 1981). Two good guides to local trees are *Northwest Trees* (The Mountaineers, 1977) and *Pacific Coast Tree Finder* (Nature Study Guild, 1973).

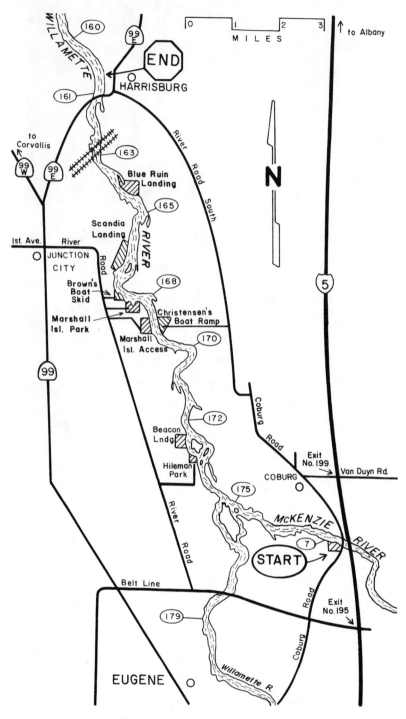

WILLAMETTE RIVER

1

Armitage Park to Harrisburg

Location: north of Eugene
Distance: 21 miles
Time: 4 hours
USGS Maps: Eugene East, Coburg, Junction City, and Harrisburg 7.5′
Best Season: all year
Rating: C

This is a fast-moving section of the Willamette and the last seven miles of the McKenzie. It begins a few miles north of Eugene and ends at the tiny town of Harrisburg.

Begin by leaving a car at the Harrisburg City Park boat ramp near the north end of Harrisburg, at the corner of First and Monroe streets. This sleepy town was once a busy port of call for steamboats plying the Willamette. It was founded in the early 1850's, and the first steamboat called in 1856. The importance of the river commerce to the town diminished in the 1870's when the railroad arrived.

The launching point is Armitage State Park, where Coburg Road and Interstate 5 cross the McKenzie north of Eugene. It can be reached from Harrisburg by following River Road South to Coburg Road.

The McKenzie and the Willamette in the Eugene area are not slow backwater sloughs. While encountering no white water, paddlers must do more than drift along enjoying the view. Wear your life jackets, and carefully watch the currents and channels. New islands and channels are constantly being created, only to be eroded away or abandoned later.

The McKenzie enters the Willamette at approximately river mile 175 of the Willamette. This same point is considered to be river mile 0 of the McKenzie, since river miles are measured from the mouth of each river. The area near this intersection is a maze of islands, and paddlers are not likely to know exactly when one river becomes the other. Unless you are particularly observant you will probably still be looking for the intersection 10 miles after you pass it. Watch for occasional river mile markers.

The numerous parks along the way would make good stopping points if you would like to plan a shorter trip. For lunch or exploring however, the public landings are preferable since they have no auto access.

Two railroad bridges are reached at mile 163, then Harrisburg appears just after passing under the Highway 99E bridge. This crossing was first served by a ferry in 1848, and then by a bridge in 1923.

The boat ramp, not easily seen from upstream, is on the right bank, at the north end of town. If the current is strong, stay close to the bank, or you will miss the ramp.

2

Harrisburg to Peoria

Location: north of Eugene
Distance: 14 miles
Time: 5 hours
USGS Maps: Harrisburg and Peoria 7.5′
Best Season: all year
Rating: B

The paddle between Harrisburg and Peoria is a fast one. Although the river winds its way around numerous large bends and past several islands, the current is very strong, even late in the year.

Begin the trip by leaving an extra car at Peoria Park just north of Peoria. If driving from the north, take I-5 Exit 228 and drive west to Tangent, then south on 99E to Shedd. If driving from the south, take Exit 216, drive west to Halsey, and then north on 99E to Shedd. From Shedd, drive west on Fayetteville Drive to Peoria.

Before the railroad attracted most of the business to neighboring Shedd and Halsey, Peoria was an important river port. The town is said to have been founded by members of the Peoria Party of 1839, a group of Illinois pioneers who had more than their share of difficulties in their journey to Oregon.

The launching point is reached by driving south on Peoria Road to Harrisburg. Launch at the boat ramp at the north end of town, at the corner of First and Monroe streets.

Between Harrisburg and Peoria, the river has a consistent pattern of S curves as it flows north. If you are in a hurry or just tired of paddling, keep to the faster water on the outside of each curve; but if you are looking for a more leisurely trip, keep to the inside shore.

Watch for sweepers. As the faster water on the outside of each turn erodes the riverbank, trees frequently fall into the river. Considerable hazard is presented to paddlers, since the current can often pull a boat under the logs.

Numerous small islands in this section give paddlers opportunities for decision making. The safest course is usually to stay in the main channel,

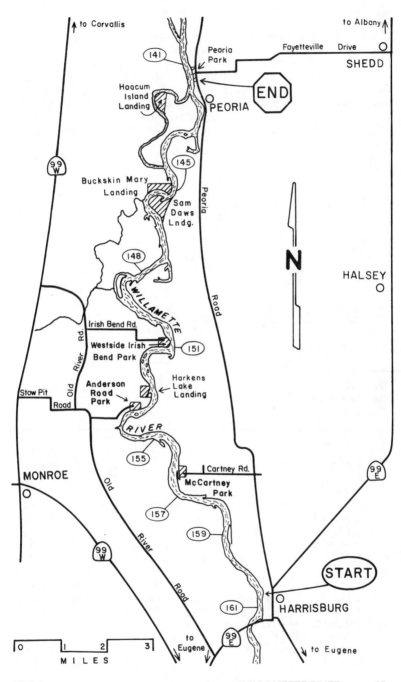

but keep a lookout for debris and shallow spots or for side channels worth exploring.

A mile marker is posted at mile 152. At mile 149, Norwood Island marks the mouth of the Long Tom River. Shortly afterwards, the river begins to slow down somewhat, as the river channel levels out and widens.

At mile 144.5, just past two public access areas marked by several river mileposts, the Albany Channel exits to the left, behind Hoacum Island. This side streambed was once the main channel of the river, but is currently navigable, if at all, only during high water. It rejoins the main channel at Peoria, a quarter mile upstream from Peoria Park, the ending point for this trip.

3

Peoria to Corvallis

Location: south of Corvallis
Distance: 10 miles
Time: 4 hours
USGS Maps: Peoria, Riverside, and Corvallis 7.5'
Best Season: all year
Rating: B

As the Willamette approaches Corvallis from Peoria, it begins its transformation from a fast-moving river with rapidly eroding banks to a slower, wider, and straighter channel. But it still moves along fairly quickly; this 10-mile section takes only a few hours.

Start this trip by leaving an extra car or a bicycle in Corvallis. From the west end of the Highway 34 bridges, drive north on Second Street, then turn right on Tyler. After one block, turn north to the boat ramp.

Then return to Highway 34 and drive east about a mile. Turn right on Peoria Road, and follow it about eight miles to Peoria Park just north of Peoria.

About a mile after launching, you will reach a fork in the river. The main channel keeps to the right, while the Bonneville Channel and Middle Channel exit on the left. The navigability of both of these side channels is open to question. If you feel adventurous, you might give one of them a try, with the understanding that portages may be required.

Unfortunately, this section of the river has only one sizable park, and landing at it is difficult. The river current past Willamette Park, at mile 134, is

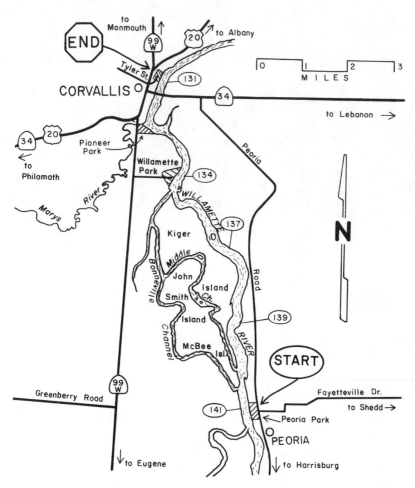

TRIP 3

fairly strong, and the bank relatively steep. The best landing spot the author could find was a tiny cove at the north end of the park.

Marys River enters the Willamette at the southern edge of Corvallis, at river mile 132 (see trip #18). If you decide to venture into its mouth (there is a public park and dock a few yards upstream), be careful, as the entrance can be shallow and rocky late in the year.

The Corvallis area is popular with boaters, particularly in speedboats. Do your best to stay out of their way, since they are in too much of a hurry to watch out for you, much less look back at the effects of their wakes.

Other types of boaters use the area, too. If you see a funny looking canoe with eight oarsmen, it is the OSU crew out for a practice session. Do not offer to race them.

Hyak Park near Albany

4

Corvallis to Albany

Location: Albany/Corvallis area
Distance: 11 miles
Time: 5 hours
USGS Maps: Corvallis, Riverside, Lewisburg, and Albany 7.5′
Best Season: all year
Rating: A

Most Oregonians associate Albany with the view they get as they roar past on the freeway. They do not look beyond the industrial section of the town, to its numerous historic buildings, much less notice that the Willamette flows through Albany and past those factories north of town.

Like many Oregon towns, Albany was named for an eastern city. At one point, its name was changed to Takenah, an Indian word describing the deep channel where the Willamette is joined by the Calapooia River; but some people interpreted the word as meaning "hole in the ground," so the name Albany was reinstated.

Start this trip by leaving an extra car at Bryant Park in Albany. The park is just west of downtown; from the west end of 3rd Avenue, cross the Calapooia River bridge and turn right towards the boat ramp. Then drive to Corvallis either on the west side of the river (use Highway 20) or stay on the east side (follow Bryant Drive south to Riverside Drive and Highway 34).

Launch your boat at the Corvallis Aquathusiasts Boat Ramp just north

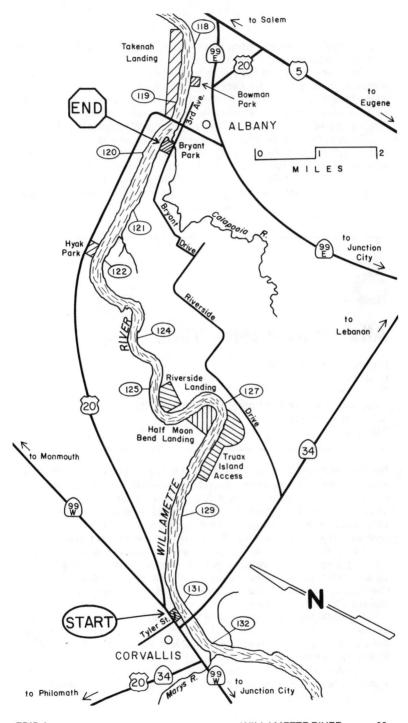

of the foot of Tyler Street, a few blocks north of the Highway 34 bridge. Be wary of speedboats in the Corvallis area.

The river is slow and fairly wide north of Corvallis, but there is no real reason to be in a hurry. Sit back and enjoy the pastoral surroundings, or watch for wildlife. In spring and summer ospreys can be seen skimming the water or diving feet first for fish. These birds, normally considered to be fairly rare, can be seen with some frequency along the Willamette in this area.

Three public access areas between miles 129 and 125 offer excellent lunch spots or campsites, but none offers drinking water. You should carry your own, but if you run out, it is available at Hyak Park at mile 122.

Bryant Park in Albany is hard to miss, sitting on a point formed by the entrance of the Calapooia River, just upstream from the Highway 20 bridges.

5

Albany to Buena Vista

Location: north of Albany
Distance: 15 miles
Time: 6 hours
USGS Maps: Albany, Lewisburg, and Monmouth 7.5′
Best Season: all year
Rating: A

The town of Buena Vista, or what is left of it, is a classic example of a town whose economic life has always been centered on the river. No main roads or highways have ever passed through it. It has never been served by a railroad, although tracks have passed within a few miles on either side of the town. Yet it was a thriving industrial center in the late nineteenth century, when its kilns were the region's only source of clay pipe and cooking ware.

Today the kilns, lumber mills, grist mills, hotels, and saloons are gone, and only a small community remains. Its only distinction is the site of the southernmost of the three remaining ferries on the Willamette. First operated by the town's founder, Reason B. Hall, the ferry has now been operating for almost 130 years.

To paddle from Albany to Buena Vista, start by leaving an extra car at Buena Vista, which can be reached by driving west from I-5 Exit 242, or from Independence by driving south on Main Street and turning left on Hartman Road (see map for trip #6).

A park and boat ramp on the west bank just south of the ferry landing is a good place to leave a car, but the east bank has parking too. The ferry does not run on weekends.

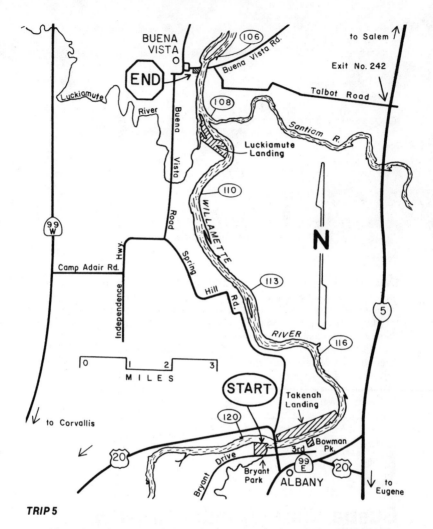

TRIP 5

If the ferry is not running, and you are parked on the west side, drive south on Buena Vista Road and Spring Hill Road to Albany. From the east side, return to Interstate 5 and proceed south to Albany.

In Albany, drive west on Third Avenue, cross the Calapooia River, and turn right into Bryant Park. The boat ramp is on the point, where the Calapooia and Willamette meet. (To paddle the Calapooia, see trip #19.)

As you pass through Albany the left (west) bank of the river for nearly two miles is all publicly owned. Since it is not accessible by car, river travelers have the area to themselves, without any screeching tires or blaring car stereos.

A similar greenway area, with campsites, occupies a mile-long bank between miles 108 and 109, where the Luckiamute enters from the west and the

Bowman Park in Albany

Santiam from the east (see trips #21 and #22). What a contrast these rivers present! The Santiam, draining 2000 square miles of foothills and mountains, enters wide and strong. By comparison, the entrance of the small and lazy Luckiamute is easy to miss. Since the current of the Luckiamute is nil, its mouth can easily be explored by canoe.

Below the mouth of the Santiam, huge white cliffs tower over the newly strengthened Willamette. Ospreys and turkey vultures circle overhead, while herons stand erect and silent on the banks.

In summer, a small floating dock on the west bank marks Buena Vista Park, near the head of Wells Island.

6

Buena Vista to Independence

Location: between Salem and Albany
Distance: 11 miles
Time: 5 hours
USGS Maps: Monmouth and Sidney 7.5′
Best Season: all year
Rating: A

The Willamette River carves a five-mile arc between Buena Vista and Independence around an area containing much history, as evidenced by its name, "American Bottom." The name derives from the days when the resi-

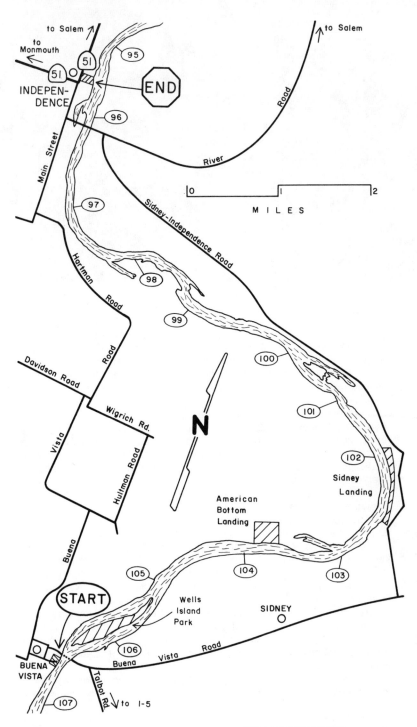

to Salem

to Monmouth

95

51   51

END

INDEPEN-
DENCE

Main Street

96

Sidney-Independence Road

River

to Salem

Road

0   1   2

M I L E S

97

Hartman

98

Road

99

Davidson Road

100

Wigrich Rd.

101

N

Vista

Hultman Road

102

Sidney
Landing

American
Bottom
Landing

103

Buena

105

104

START

Wells
Island
Park

SIDNEY

BUENA
VISTA

106

Buena   Vista   Road

Talbot Rd.

to I-5

107

Buena Vista ferry

dents of the Oregon region were evenly divided between Americans and French-Canadians. The Canadians were concentrated in "French Prairie" near St. Paul, while the Americans had "American Bottom."

Independence seems relatively untouched by the passage of time. Named for a Missouri river town, its historic architecture is clearly visible even as one approaches by water.

Start this trip by leaving an extra car in Independence, at Polk Marine Park at the foot of South B Street. Independence can be reached from Salem by following River Road south. From Albany, Independence can be reached by driving to Buena Vista up the west side of the Willamette using the map accompanying trip #5, and then continuing west of the river by the route marked on the map for this trip.

After depositing your vehicle, drive south from Independence on Main Street. About a mile out of town, turn left on Hartman Road, and follow it (and several signs) to Buena Vista. Launch your boat at the county park just south of the ferry landing. The ferry does not run on weekends.

Wells Island lies in the river just north of the ferry route. A mile long, the island is a county park with facilities for camping and picnicking. Water is not available on the island, but can be brought over from Buena Vista Park.

Below Wells Island, the Willamette is wide and smooth. Near the east bank lies the community of Sidney. Under the name of Ankeny's Landing, the Sidney area was once the major fuel yard of the upper Willamette, where steamboats could lay in a fresh supply of cordwood. Just east of here lies Ankeny National Wildlife Refuge, a large federal reserve devoted primarily to the preservation of wintering grounds for a subspecies of Canada geese, the dusky Canada goose.

After passing one more large island, the river turns north, and the Independence bridge comes into view. A large floating dock on the left bank marks the end of the trip.

7

Independence to Salem

Location: south of Salem
Distance: 12 miles
Time: 5 hours
USGS Maps: Monmouth, Rickreal, and Salem West 7.5′
Best Season: all year
Rating: A

Between Independence and Salem, the Willamette makes several wide bends around Hayden Island, Browns Island, and Minto Island, none of which are true islands. As the Willamette has changed its course over the last 150 years, the channels behind islands named by early settlers dried up and left only disconnected sloughs, crescent-shaped lakes, and large non-islands.

Wallace Marine Park in Salem

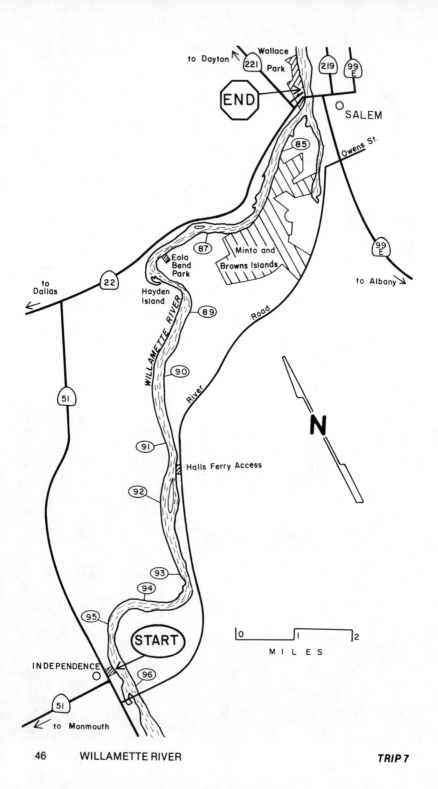

The trip from Independence begins in Salem, when you leave an extra car or bicycle at Wallace Marine Park, located under the west ends of the Highway 22 bridges. Then drive, with your boat, south to Independence. The west side drive is probably the fastest (follow Highway 22 west to Highway 51 and turn south), but the east side is more scenic (from downtown Salem, drive south on Commercial Street, turn left on Owens Street, and follow it as it becomes River Road). In Independence, launch from Polk Marine Park, at the foot of South B Street.

Shortly after the launching, the river makes a broad S curve towards a large unnamed island at mile 92. The tiny community of Halls Ferry is located behind the island on the right bank. The site of the former ferry landing is located downstream, near mile 91, and is today a small public access area. Watch for a river mile marker. The owner and operator of the ferry in the 1880's was B.F. Hall, son of the founder and ferry operator of Buena Vista, 15 miles upstream.

Commercial marinas are located at mile 88 (near the mouth of Rickreal Creek) and mile 85.

Two of the largest "non-islands," Browns Island and Minto Island, occupy the right bank and are now public parks operated by Marion County and the city of Salem.

The only bridges on the trip, the dual bridges of Highway 22 in Salem, mark its end. Wallace Marine Park, under their west ends, is extremely popular with powerboats, so be careful when landing.

8

Salem to Wheatland Ferry

Location: north of Salem
Distance: 12 miles
Time: 5 hours
USGS Maps: Salem West and Mission Bottom 7.5'
Best Season: all year
Rating: A

The 12-mile paddle from Salem to Wheatland is a particularly pleasant trip. It offers smooth paddling, a gentle current, several public access areas to explore, and some interesting history.

Originally named Atchison, Wheatland was first settled in 1844 by Daniel Matheny, who took up the noble professions of farming, operating a ferry, and selling property in his future town. As of this writing, the current ferry, the *Daniel Matheny IV*, still runs seven days a week, although a toll has recently been added.

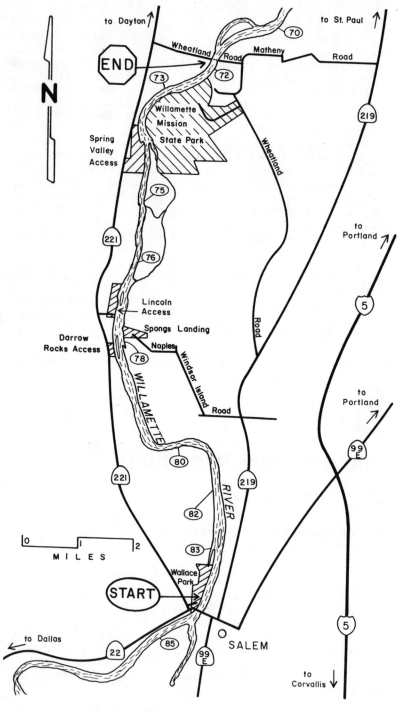

to Dayton

to St. Paul

70

Wheatland   Road   Matheny   Road

END

73

72

219

Willamette
Mission
State Park

Spring
Valley
Access

Wheatland

75

to Portland

221

76

Road

5

Lincoln
Access

Spongs Landing

Darrow
Rocks Access

Naples

78

Windsor Island

to
Portland

WILLAMETTE

Road

80

99
E

221

219

82

RIVER

83

0   1   2
M I L E S

Wallace
Park

START

to Dallas

22   85

99
E

SALEM

5

to
Corvallis

Across the river, on the east bank, was the site of Jason Lee's Methodist Mission, which Lee abandoned in 1840 in favor of a site 12 miles upstream. The Indians had named the new site Chemeketa, but in 1844, the same year Wheatland was settled, the missionaries renamed the town Salem and began marketing lots.

To paddle through this historic area now known as Mission Bottom, leave an extra car on either side of the river at the Wheatland ferry crossing. The ferry can be reached from Interstate 5 by driving east from Exit 271 (Woodburn) or 263 (Brooks). Then drive south to Salem. On the east side, follow Matheny Road and Wheatland Road to Highway 219 and continue south to Salem. In Salem, turn west on Highway 22 (Marion Street) and cross the river. If starting from the west side of the ferry, drive to Highway 221 and turn south. The launching point is the public boat ramp at Wallace Marine Park, under the west ends of the Highway 22 bridges.

The river passes several islands at mile 83 and mile 80. At mile 79.5, where the river turns sharply north, beware of Rice Rocks, which may be hidden just below the surface of the water near the left bank; the right bank is much safer.

At mile 77, the east bank is (or perhaps was) known as Lincoln, while the west bank is named Spongs Landing, after a ferry operator of the late 1800's. Today the landing is a county park.

Windsor Island lies along the east bank between miles 76 and 74. The main channel once passed on the east side of this island, but today the main channel is on the west side, and the east channel is all but abandoned.

A similar "island," Beaver Island, occurs between miles 73 and 72. On the east bank of the former channel, now known as Mission Lake, is the former site of Jason Lee's mission, now a large state park.

9

Wheatland Ferry to St. Paul

Location: St. Paul area
Distance: 15 miles
Time: 4 to 6 hours
USGS Maps: Mission Bottom and Dayton 7.5′
Best Season: all year
Rating: A

The Willamette River from Wheatland to St. Paul provides one of the area's most popular canoe trips. The current is steady, the scenery pleasant, and the river winds its way past several interesting islands. The largest of these is Grand Island, nearly five miles long. On its west side is Lambert Slough, an adventurous variation to this trip.

A folding kayak along the banks of the Lambert Slough

Start by leaving an extra car at San Salvador County Park near St. Paul. To get there, drive west from St. Paul on Blanchet Avenue, which becomes Horseshoe Lake Road, and then turns to gravel before it reaches the park. Then drive south from St. Paul through Fairfield and turn right onto Highway 219. One-quarter mile past the community of Concomly, turn right on Matheny Road and follow it four miles to the park next to the ferry landing.

The Lambert Slough variation leaves the main channel of the Willamette almost immediately after the launch. Look for a row of pilings on the left bank, then paddle through an opening in this barrier to a slough behind Wheatland Bar. A half mile later (including some shallow spots), the Lambert Slough can be reached by portaging over Wheatland Dam at a low point near its north end.

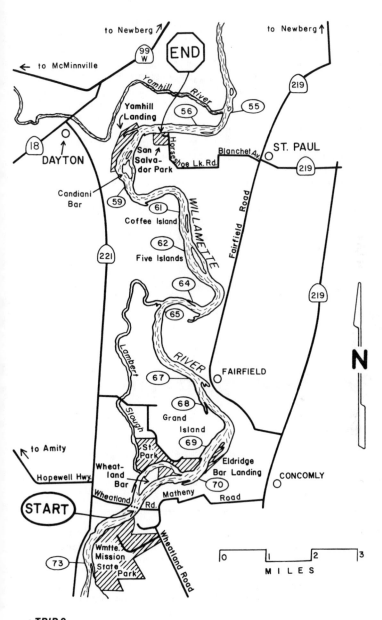

TRIP 9

This variation is not recommended except early in the year, and only to those willing to put up with numerous shallow spots and some brushy paddling. The reward, as you might guess, is a shady, secluded journey. While the northern half of the slough is free of obstructions, the southern half has numerous passages that will require lining the boats through shallow areas or fighting your way through brush or reeds and grasses. One or two parts will require a portage. In the opinion of the author, the effort is worth it, but you might not agree. If it sounds to your liking, choose a warm spring day, an old pair of sneakers, and an adventurous friend.

For the less adventurous, stay in the main channel, or, after paddling through the pilings near the ferry, stay in this two-mile slough until it rejoins the main channel.

The Willamette has been very active in this part of its journey north, carving numerous islands and sloughs only to abandon them, leaving crescent-shaped lakes, inlets, and gravel bars. At several points, dikes and dams have been built to minimize the wandering tendency. Dams at the southern ends of Wheatland Bar, Grand Island, Five Islands, Coffee Island, and Candiani Bar are all examples of such preventive construction, and the sloughs behind them make attractive detours.

10

St. Paul to Champoeg Park

Location: Newberg area
Distance: 11 miles
Time: 5 hours
USGS Maps: Dayton, St. Paul, and Newberg 7.5'
NOAA Chart: #18528
Best Season: all year
Rating: A

This 11-mile section of the Willamette curves around the northwest corner of French Prairie, a hundred square-mile area of small towns and farmland that has played a central role in Oregon's history. First inhabited by Kalapooian Indians, its current name is derived from the French-Canadians who settled in the area after retiring from the Hudson's Bay Company. Today its small towns have retained much of their charm, and many of the Victorian farmhouses of the area have survived their first century.

Start this trip by leaving an extra car or bicycle at Champoeg State Park, reached from Interstate 5 by driving west from Exit 278 or 282, as shown on the map accompanying trip #11. After entering the park, follow the signs to

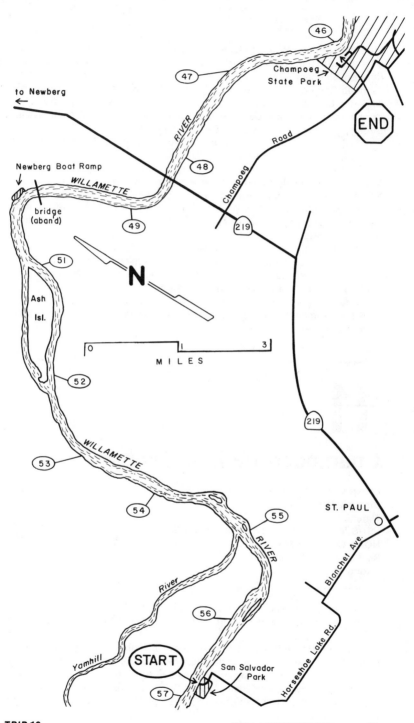

to Newberg

Newberg Boat Ramp

WILLAMETTE

bridge
(aban'd)

46

47

Champoeg
State Park

END

48

Champoeg   Road

49

219

51

N

Ash
Isl.

0   1   3

M I L E S

52

53

WILLAMETTE

219

54

55

ST. PAUL

River

RIVER

56

Blanchet Ave.

START

San Salvador
Park

Harseshoe Lake Rd.

57

Yamhill

River

RIVER

the D.A.R. Pioneer Mothers Memorial Cabin, and leave your car near it. Then drive west from the park to Highway 219, and follow it south to St. Paul. Turn right on Blanchet Avenue, but slow down to admire the imposing St. Paul Catholic Church, and try to imagine what French Prairie was like in 1846 when the church was built to replace a log chapel. Follow Blanchet Avenue as it becomes Horseshoe Lake Road then turns to gravel as it passes through hop fields on its way to San Salvador Park.

The river, wide and smooth, is joined by the sluggish Yamhill River two miles after the launch site. (See trips #23 and #24.) At river mile 52, Ash Island divides the river. Both channels are navigable, but if powerboats are out in force, as they usually are on summer weekends, take the relatively secluded left channel by paddling through a row of pilings.

In the right-hand channel, a private ferry at mile 52.5 shuttles farm equipment and crops between the island and the east bank. The island is private property.

A mile downstream, near a public boat ramp, local industry and a large abandoned bridge dominate the skyline. After passing under the bridge, stay away from the left bank for the next quarter mile or so, unless you are conducting some sort of sewage-treatment study.

Champoeg Park is easy to miss. Watch for a small clearing on the right bank then a small floating dock a few feet downstream. Your car or bicycle is a short walk east from the dock.

11

Champoeg Park to Canby

Location: Wilsonville area
Distance: 10 miles
Time: 5 hours
USGS Maps: Newberg, Sherwood, and Canby 7.5′
NOAA Chart: #18528
Best Season: all year
Rating: A

This is a straightforward section of the Willamette, but one filled with history and wildlife. It starts at the site of the former town of Champoeg, now a state park.

The trip also ends at a state park. Leave an extra car at the Molalla River State Park on the south side of the Willamette, a half mile west of the Canby Ferry. Then drive southwest on Highway 99E to Aurora. Turn right on Main Street, and follow it as it becomes Ehlen Road then Yergen Road after crossing Butteville Road. Drive another 3.5 miles, turn right on Case Road, and go

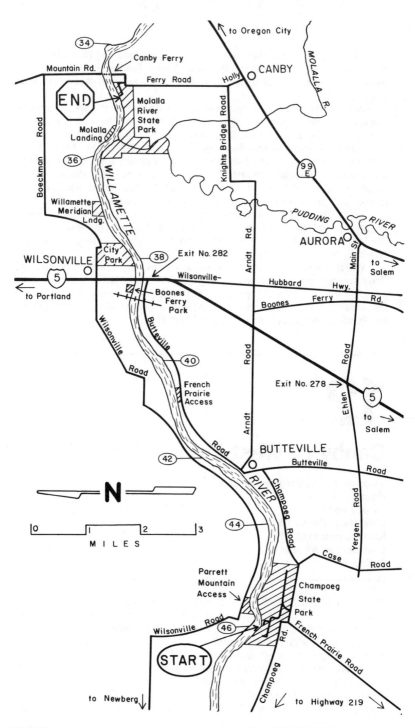

to Oregon City

34

Mountain Rd.
Canby Ferry

CANBY

Ferry Road
Holly

END

Molalla
River
State
Park

Boeckman Road

Molalla
Landing

36

Knights Bridge Road

MOLALLA R.

99 E

Willamette
Meridian
Lndg.

PUDDING RIVER

WILLAMETTE

AURORA

to Salem

WILSONVILLE

City
Park

38

Exit No. 282

5

Wilsonville-

Hubbard Hwy.

Main St.

to Portland

Boones
Ferry
Park

Butteville

40

Boones Ferry Rd.

Wilsonville Road

French
Prairie
Access

Arndt Road

Exit No. 278

5

to Salem

Ehlen Road

Road

42

RIVER

BUTTEVILLE

Butteville Road

N

Arndt Road

Champoeg Road

Yergen Road

0 1 2 3
M I L E S

44

Case Road

Parrett
Mountain
Access

Champoeg
State
Park

Wilsonville Road

46

French Prairie Road

Champoeg Rd.

START

to Newberg

to Highway 219

to Champoeg Road. Turn left, then enter the state park and follow the signs to the D.A.R. Pioneer Mothers Memorial Cabin. From the turnaround just west of the museum, carry your boat west a few hundred feet to the boat dock.

In the early 1800's, Champoeg was the main port for the area south of it known as French Prairie. By 1843, when 102 settlers met to form a government for the Oregon territory, Champoeg was a sizable cluster of buildings centered on a street named Napoleon Boulevard. The names of the 52 men that voted for the creation of an American government are now inscribed on an obelisk in the park. Their town, however, was twice destroyed by the floods of 1861 and 1890. Today, the level of the 1861 flood is shown by a marker a dozen feet up the side of the memorial pavilion.

From Champoeg, the Willamette travels east in a slow path toward Wilsonville and the huge bridges of Interstate 5. Just west of these bridges is the former site of Boones Ferry. This part of the river is referred to as "the Newberg Pool"; don't count on much current.

Watch for wildlife, however, particularly near the mouth of the Molalla River around mile 36. One of the largest heron rookeries in the state is located on the east side of the Molalla's mouth. Unfortunately, powerboats in this area often mar the tranquility of the scene. The Molalla and its tributary, the Pudding, are discussed in trips #25 and #26.

12

Canby to West Linn

Location: Canby-Oregon City area
Distance: 7 miles
Time: 3 hours
USGS Map: Canby 7.5′
NOAA Chart: #18528
Best Season: all year
Rating: A

The seven-mile stretch of the Willamette between the mouths of the Molalla and Tualatin rivers is a pleasant reminder that portions of the river, even close to industrial centers such as Oregon City, can still be secluded. This is a short section which could conceivably be paddled in a long summer's evening, although a more leisurely trip is justified.

Leave an extra car at Willamette Park at the foot of 12th Street in the Willamette section of West Linn, which is located 2.5 miles southwest of West Linn on Highway 212 or I-205. Then cross the Tualatin River on the nearby bridge, and drive south on Pete's Mountain Road to the Canby Ferry.

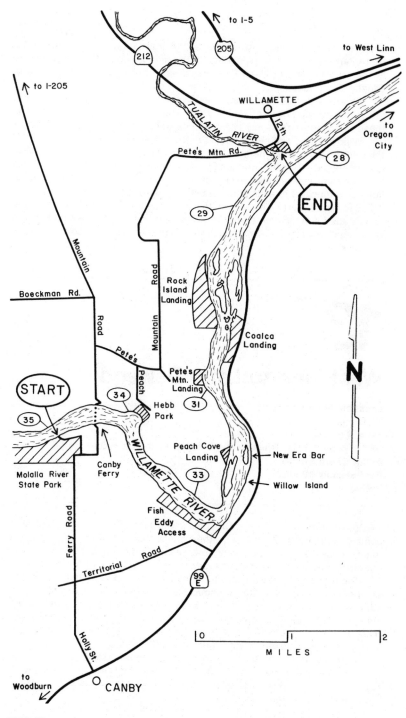

to I-5

212

205

to West Linn

to I-205

WILLAMETTE

TUALATIN RIVER

12th

to Oregon City

Pete's Mtn. Rd.

28

29

END

Mountain

Boeckman Rd.

Road

Pete's

Mountain

Road

Peach

Rock Island Landing

Coalca Landing

START

34

35

Hebb Park

Pete's Mtn. Landing

31

N

Canby Ferry

Molalla River State Park

WILLAMETTE RIVER

Peach Cove Landing

New Era Bar

33

Willow Island

Fish Eddy Access

Ferry Road

Territorial Road

99 E

0   1   2

MILES

Holly St.

to Woodburn

CANBY

TRIP 12

WILLAMETTE RIVER   57

Cross the ferry, and launch your boat at the gravel ramp at the Molalla River State Park west of the ferry landing. (If the ferry is not operating, launching at the ferry landing or Hebb Park would save driving to the Wilsonville or Oregon City bridges.)

Shortly after your launching, the river turns to the southeast at Walnut Eddy, then abruptly north at Fish Eddy. The river is quite deep at each of these turns, but is relatively shallow in between and near Willow Island.

Willow Island and nearby New Era Bar are excellent spots to watch for the wildlife, particularly herons, that feed in shallow areas. If the water level is high enough, try paddling behind these islands.

The same is true of the several small islands near Rock Island. The proximity of Highway 99E makes this area a popular fishing spot.

Soon the Tualatin enters from the left, under the bridge to Pete's Mountain Road. If you have time to spare, venture (carefully) up the Tualatin (you will not get very far) or downstream towards the Oregon City Locks, but don't get too close to the falls.

13

West Linn to Lake Oswego

Location: West Linn area
Distance: 7 miles
Time: 4 hours
USGS Maps: Canby, Oregon City, Gladstone, and Lake Oswego 7.5'
NOAA Chart: #18528
Best Season: all year
Rating: A

The installation of the Oregon City Locks was a major event in the history of commerce and transportation on the Willamette. Previously, shipments of grain, lumber, and livestock were portaged around the falls at Oregon City, but since 1872 traffic has been barged through the locks with little delay.

The first step in making this trip is to call the Locks at (503) 656-3381 to determine if they are available for small pleasure craft. During weekdays and some weekends, barge and log raft traffic may preclude recreational traffic. On these days, you have the choice of hitching a ride on a barge or raft (not recommended!), or carrying your boat along the half mile length of the locks (ditto), or waiting till another day (much better).

The next step is to leave an extra car at George Rogers Park in Lake Oswego near the intersection of McVey Avenue and State Street (Highway 43). Glance at the huge chimney from the old blast furnace so you will know when to stop paddling.

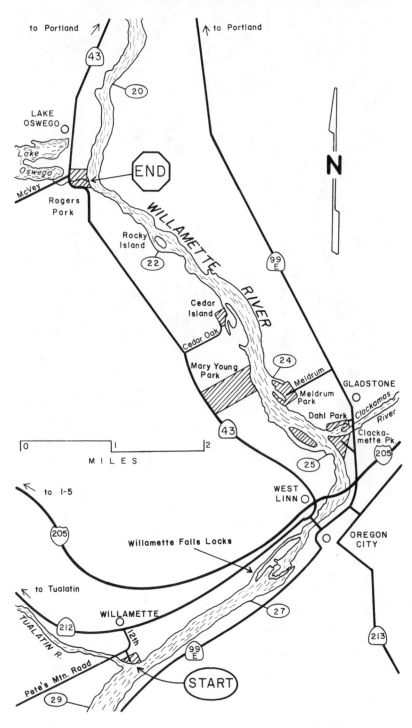

to Portland ↑
to Portland ↑

43

20

N

LAKE
OSWEGO ○

Lake
Oswego

McVey

Rogers
Park

END

99
E

WILLAMETTE

Rocky
Island

22

RIVER

Cedar
Island

Cedar Oak

Mary Young
Park

24

Meldrum

Meldrum
Park

GLADSTONE ○

Clackamas
River

Dahl Park

Clacka-
mette Pk.

43

0   1   2
M I L E S

25

205

← to I-5

WEST
LINN ○

205

OREGON
CITY ○

Willamette Falls Locks

← to Tualatin

TUALATIN R.

212

WILLAMETTE ○

12th

27

213

99
E

Pete's Mtn. Road

START

29

Canby Ferry

Start the trip at the mouth of the Tualatin River, at the large park at the foot of 12th Street in the community of Willamette, 2.5 miles south of West Linn on Highway 212.

Once in the river, stay near the left bank to enter the locks, and unless the lock tenders see you, look for the intercom phone to let them know they have a customer. In each chamber of the locks (oftentimes the first chamber is left open), you will be handed a rope to hold onto as the water level falls. Do *not* tie your boat to the rope, unless you want to be high and dry. There is no charge to use the locks.

After the locks, the Clackamas River joins the Willamette from the east. A mile later, Mary S. Young State Park is on the left near a rocky outcropping. After another mile is Cedar Island (which is neither an island nor populated by cedars), and a popular public boat ramp near its north end.

At mile 22 is accurately named Rocky Island, and a mile farther the Oswego blast furnace is visible next to Oswego Creek.

14

Lake Oswego to Willamette Park

Location: Portland area
Distance: 5 miles
Time: 2 to 3 hours
USGS Map: Lake Oswego 7.5′
NOAA Chart: #18528
Best Season: all year
Rating: A

The paddle from Lake Oswego's Rogers Park to Portland's Willamette Park is short but scenic, and an island park halfway along is worth at least a short layover.

Start by leaving an extra car at Willamette Park off Macadam Avenue (Highway 43) in Portland. Or consider returning to the starting point by bus.

Oregon City Locks

Near Powers Marine Park

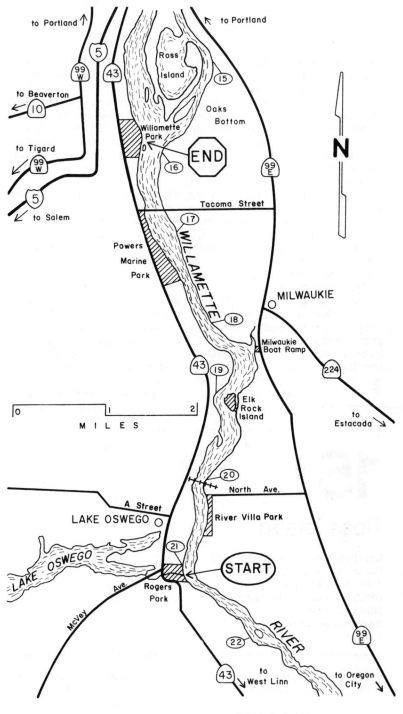

to Portland ↑

to Portland ↗

Ross Island

Oaks Bottom

5

99 W

43

to Beaverton

10

to Tigard

99 W

5

to Salem

15

Willamette Park

16

END

99 E

Tacoma Street

17

Powers Marine Park

WILLAMETTE

18

MILWAUKIE

Milwaukie Boat Ramp

43

19

224

to Estacada

0   1   2

M I L E S

Elk Rock Island

20

North Ave.

A Street

LAKE OSWEGO

River Villa Park

LAKE OSWEGO

21

Ave.

Rogers Park

START

McVey

22

RIVER

99 E

43

to West Linn

to Oregon City

N

Tri-Met bus line #36 runs south along Macadam Avenue to the put-in spot, George Rogers Park, at the intersection of McVey Avenue and State Street (Highway 43) in Lake Oswego.

The town of Oswego had its beginnings on this site in 1850 when a water-powered sawmill was built on the banks of what was then called Sucker Creek. A decade later, iron deposits were found in the neighboring hills, and in 1867 iron works were erected. Several steamboats were also built on this site for use in Lake Oswego and the Tualatin River. Eventually low iron prices and low water on the Tualatin put an end to the latter two activities.

One mile past the launching site, the river passes under a railroad bridge, and another mile later it narrows as it passes Elk Rock Island. An island only at high water, this peninsula is a city park that is accessible only by boat or (at low water) by foot. A tiny beach in a small cove on the west side of the island makes an excellent landing spot for lunch, exploration, or napping on the rocks. A primitive trail circles the island, and an old shelter stands near the east side.

Powers Marine Park, at mile 17, sees heavy use in the summer. Unfortunately, the rest of the Willamette in Portland is not lined with similar parks.

Oaks Bottom, on the east side of the river just north of the Sellwood Bridge, is an example of the flood plains that once lined the Willamette. Most of the flood plains have been diked, drained, and developed, and are no longer available to reduce the severity of spring floods. Although separated from the river by an amusement park and a dike, Oaks Bottom is one of the few flood plains that continues to serve its natural purpose.

This entire section of the Willamette is narrow in places and is also popular with powerboats. Stay close to one bank or the other to avoid them.

15

Ross Island

Location: near downtown Portland
Distance: 2 to 4 miles
Time: up to 4 hours
USGS Map: Lake Oswego 7.5′
NOAA Chart: #18528
Best Season: all year
Rating: A

The large island in the Willamette River just south of Ross Island Bridge was once two islands, Hardtack Island and its neighbor to the north, Ross Island.

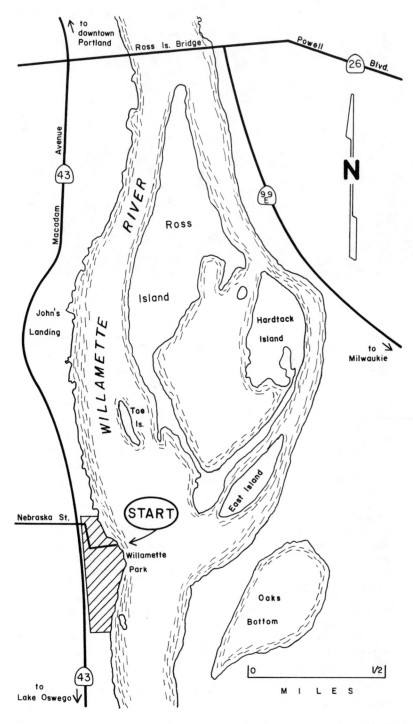

to downtown Portland

Ross Is. Bridge

Powell Blvd.

26

Avenue

43

Macadam

9.9 E

N

RIVER

Ross

Island

WILLAMETTE

John's Landing

Hardtack Island

to Milwaukie

Toe Is.

East Island

Nebraska St.

START

Willamette Park

Oaks Bottom

0   1/2

M I L E S

43

to Lake Oswego

Ross Island

These islands have been connected with a man-made causeway, creating a large interior lake.

Ross Island was named for Sherry Ross, who lived there in the late 1800's. Mr. Ross reportedly met his wife on a ferry as it steamed past the island. When he noticed her admiring the wooded island, Ross spoke up, pointing out that if she wanted the island, she'd have to take him too. She did.

The island's easy access makes it ideal for a short trip. A summer evening provides adequate time to completely circle the island and to explore its interior lake.

Start the trip at Willamette Park. The park entrance is located at the corner of Nebraska Street and Macadam Avenue in southwest Portland.

The wide portion of the river just off the park is a popular place for powerboats, both commercial vessels and recreational speedboats. Cautious paddlers should limit their exposure here by paddling directly across the river to the south end of Hardtack Island.

During periods of high water, the quiet slough on the far side of the islands can be reached by paddling on either side of East Island. During low water (and low tide), the deeper channel on the far side of East Island is best. During extremely low water, stay close to the houseboats at the Oregon Yacht Club.

Away from the roar of most of the river traffic, the channel behind the islands offers relative quiet and a chance to observe some wildlife. Watch for beaver and for the great blue herons that nest on Ross Island.

In 1912, the city of Portland sought voter approval of a plan to build a Ross Island Bridge, similar to the one that now spans the river, but with connecting bridges to both Ross and Hardtack islands. The plan called for boulevards and public promenades on Ross Island, with a "public incinerator and workshops for city prisoners" on Hardtack Island. While the park plan may have been a bit grandiose (and unusual), the islands' present condition is deplorable, the result of dredging and excavating by the Ross Island Sand and Gravel Company. Even worse, the company plans to expand its operations on the islands.

The circumnavigation of the islands can be made by continuing around the north end of Ross Island into the main channel of the river. Once in the main channel, stay close to one bank or the other to avoid powerboats that, like gravel companies, make less than ideal rivermates.

16

Willamette Park to Swan Island

Location: Portland
Distance: 9 miles
Time: 5 hours
USGS Maps: Lake Oswego and Portland 7.5′
NOAA Chart: #18526
Best Season: all year
Rating: A

The Willamette River undergoes dramatic changes as it passes through the city of Portland. On the southern edge of town, it is almost rural in character, thanks to wooded banks and extensive parks such as Powers Park and Oaks Bottom. After passing through the city, however, the river is almost entirely industrialized, with huge grain elevators, public wharfs, and containerized shipping terminals.

The launching point for this trip is the city's Willamette Park, the entrance to which is at the intersection of S.W. Nebraska Street and Highway 43 (Macadam Avenue). On a spring or summer day, you can expect Willamette Park to be swarming with people, cars, and boat trailers.

The ending point, where you should leave an extra car, is the public boat ramp at Swan Island, easily reached by driving west on Going Street from Interstate 5 Exit 303. The ramp is on Lagoon Avenue, at its intersection with Ballast Street.

After launching from Willamette Park, you might consider paddling around the far side of Ross Island to avoid some of the powerboat traffic. See trip #15 for a discussion of Ross Island.

Just west of Ross Island, the John's Landing area is being redeveloped. Once the domain of lumber mills and furniture factories, the west bank is now being built up with condominiums, apartments, restaurants, and office buildings. With each new development, the city has been requiring the developers to build public bicycle and pedestrian paths along the river.

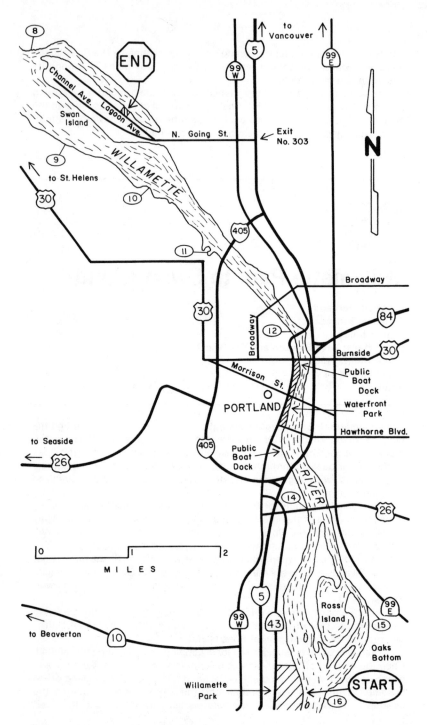

Someday the paths will link Willamette Park and Powers Park with the downtown waterfront.

This trip paddles under eight bridges. From south to north, they are the Ross Island, the Marquam (I-5), the Hawthorne, the Morrison, the Burnside, the Steel, the Broadway, and the Fremont (I-405) bridges. Of the eight, the huge arches of the Fremont are the most grand and the piers of the Marquam are the ugliest, but the most intricate is the Steel Bridge, with its double-deck auto and railroad drawspans that can be operated independently.

The endpoint for this urban paddle is on the west side of the Swan Island Lagoon, which can be entered at mile 8 near the dry docks. Be careful of industrial boat traffic in the Swan Island area.

17

Swan Island to Kelley Point

Location: north of Portland
Distance: 9 miles
Time: 5 hours
USGS Maps: Portland, Linnton, and Sauvie Island 7.5′
NOAA Chart: #18526
Best Season: all year
Rating: A

Swan Island has always played an important role in the development of Portland. In the 1850's, when several embryo towns were competing for the role of the regional center of shipping and commerce, difficulties in crossing the Swan Island sand bar were downplayed by Portlanders, while downstream rivals exaggerated the hazards of crossing the bar during periods of low water.

Swan Island even played a role when the age of air travel began. In the 1920's, Swan Island was selected as the site of a municipal airport, and a causeway was built to the east shore out of dredgings from the west channel. The airport was barely completed in time to host a 1927 visit by Charles Lindberg.

The trip described here starts at the public boat ramp on the former east channel of the river and paddles nine miles downstream to the mouth of the Willamette at Kelley Point. The park at Kelley Point, where an extra car should be left, can be reached from Interstate 5 Exit 307 by driving west on Marine Drive.

From Kelley Point, return to Interstate 5 and drive south to Exit 303. Drive west on Going Street, and turn right on Lagoon Avenue to the boat ramp near the intersection of Lagoon Avenue and Ballast Street.

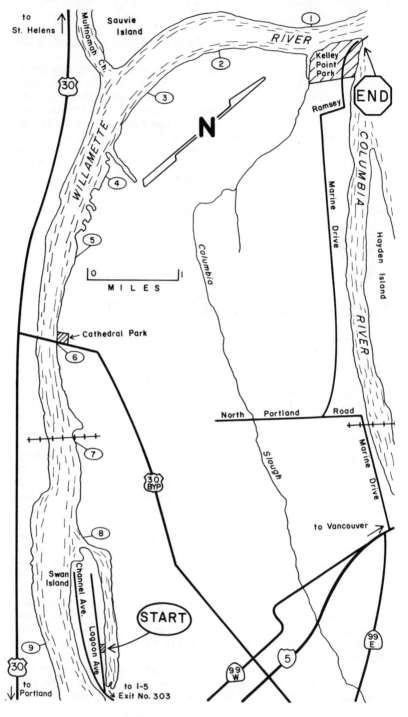

Cathedral Park under the St. Johns Bridge

On entering the main channel of the Willamette, the first major landmark consists of the huge Port of Portland dry docks on the north end of Swan Island, among the largest on the west coast. Keep them in mind next time your boat needs repairs.

The University of Portland stands on the bluff just north of the dry docks, and across the river is the Port tanker basin, home of several petroleum depots. Only two bridges cross this section of the river, a railroad swing bridge at mile 7 and the St. Johns Bridge at mile 6.

The St. Johns Bridge stands as a model of what bridges ought to look like. Built in 1929-1930 at a cost of $4 million, its thousand foot span was for years the longest and highest (205 feet) of its type. The beautiful gothic towers recently inspired the naming of a new city park under the bridge's east end, Cathedral Park.

The Willamette ends its long journey at Kelley Point Park. The parking lot is a short portage from the river. Land your boat either on the west side of the point, or paddle around the jetty to the Columbia side, but watch out for other boat traffic, both small and large.

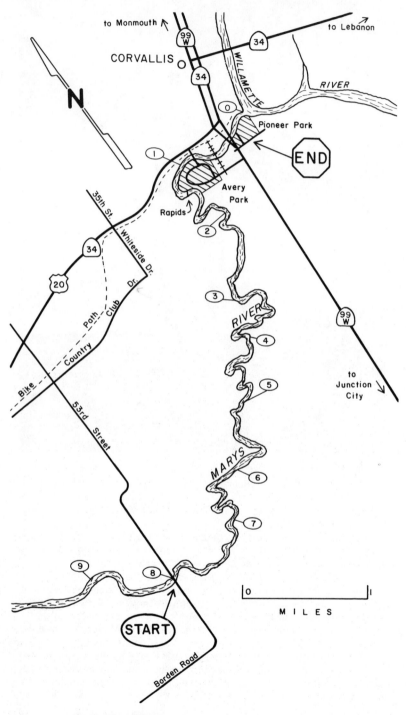

to Monmouth

to Lebanon

99 W

CORVALLIS

34

34

WILLAMETTE

RIVER

0

Pioneer Park

END

1

Avery Park

Rapids

35th St.

Whiteside Dr.

34

20

Path

Country Club Dr.

Bike

53rd Street

2

3

RIVER

4

99 W

5

to Junction City

MARYS

6

7

9

8

START

Borden Road

0 1

MILES

TRIBUTARIES OF THE WILLAMETTE RIVER

18

Marys River

Location: Corvallis
Distance: 8 miles
Time: 4 hours
USGS Map: Corvallis 7.5′
Best Season: winter and spring
Rating: A

Marys River is a small meandering stream that enters the Willamette on the southern edge of Corvallis. Due to its size, it is best paddled in winter or spring. Its smallness also means that it is easily clogged. Don't take this trip unless you are willing to work your way around (or through) an occasional small logjam.

Start this trip by leaving an extra car or bicycle at the Pioneer Park boat ramp just south of Corvallis, which is reached from the center of the city by driving south on Highway 99W. One block after crossing the Marys River bridge, turn left on Crystal Lake Road, then turn left again to the boat ramp.

This trip is particularly suited to the use of a bike as return transportation, since a bike path follows Highway 34 between Corvallis and Philomath. Look for it under the north end of the Highway 99W bridge.

The launching point is reached by driving north back over the river and taking the first left, then driving west on Highway 34 about 2.5 miles to 53rd Street. Turn left and drive 2.25 miles to a bridge over Marys River. If you left a bike at the boat ramp, note where the bike path crosses 53rd Street. The best launching is under the north end of the bridge.

The launching site, like the rest of the trip, is fairly muddy. As far as the author knows, muddy riverbanks have only one advantage: animal tracks are abundant. Watch for the tracks of beaver, muskrat, nutria, deer, and especially raccoon.

The first half of the trip may be interrupted when trees, collapsed from erosion, create small logjams. These blockages are neither numerous nor difficult to surmount. In the second half of this trip, the river widens and obstacles are left behind. A golf course is passed at mile 2.5. Farther downstream, the cement abutments of an old millrace stand on the east bank.

After mile 1.5, the remainder of the trip skirts Avery City Park. One obstacle presents itself in the park. At river mile 1.25, a large set of rapids blocks the river. When you hear them, head for the right bank, where a rock

Logjam on Marys River

walkway makes portaging easy. Do not paddle these rapids unless you are experienced in white water and have inspected them carefully from shore. In the last mile, pass four bridges. The Pioneer boat ramp is on the right, halfway between the fourth bridge and the broad waters of the Willamette. If you paddle out onto the Willamette, beware of rocks in the mouth of Marys River.

19

Calapooia River

Location: Albany
Distance: 9.5 miles
Time: 4 to 5 hours
USGS Maps: Riverside, Tangent, Lewisburg, and Albany 7.5'
Best Season: winter and spring
Rating: A

The Calapooia River is a small tributary of the Willamette, originating on the western slopes of the Cascades between the Santiam and McKenzie rivers. It joins the Willamette at Albany and was named for a group of Indians that inhabited the region. A relatively narrow and flat river, it is best paddled in winter or spring.

The trip is started by leaving an extra car in Bryant Park in Albany. From downtown Albany, drive west on 3rd Avenue, cross the Calapooia River Bridge, and turn right into the park.

When leaving the park, turn right and drive west, then south, on Bryant Drive to Riverside Drive. Turn left, then turn right on Oakville Road. About four miles farther, turn left on Highway 34. Shortly after crossing the Calapooia, turn right and park next to (or under) the bridge.

As the crow flies, your launching point under the bridge is only five miles from Albany, but the Calapooia River follows a leisurely undulating course of almost twice that distance. Even so, the river never seems content with its existing channel. The current may seem slow, but it constantly works on its banks, devouring pastures in directions it wants to travel, while leaving gravel bars in places it has been. Neighboring farmers are fighting erosion by depositing old car bodies in a few strategic locations; a course in identifying cars of the 40's and 50's could easily be taught from a canoe on the Calapooia.

The author's most memorable experience on the Calapooia began one January day when he sighted a nutria on a muddy bank. (Similar in appearance to a muskrat, but about twice as large, nutria became residents of western Oregon after escaping from financially unsuccessful fur farms.) Upon closer examination, the animal modestly hid in a clump of branches and twigs at the water's edge. In an attempt to seduce him into posing for the camera, the author gently applied a canoe paddle to his refuge. The response was immediate. Two furry projectiles, each consisting of not less than 10 pounds of airborne nutria, exploded from the brush. In the style of a berserk torpedo, the first collided with the side of the canoe well above the waterline. The second landed in shallow water near the bow of the boat with the grace of a depth charge. It has yet to be determined who was more frightened, the two nutria or the two canoe paddlers.

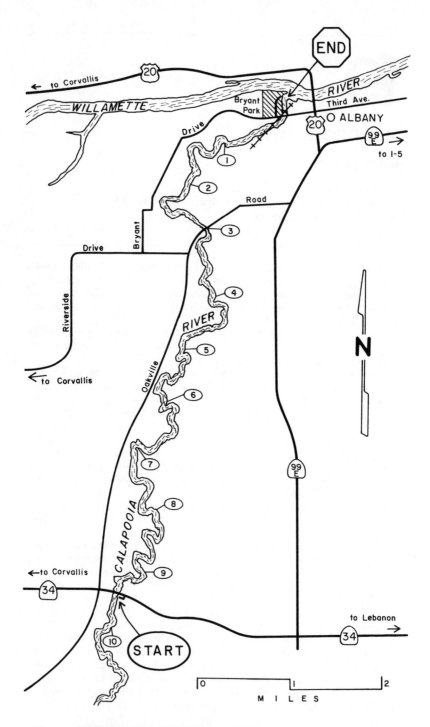

The end of the trip, Bryant Park, is marked by two railroad bridges and a highway bridge. Under the latter, the man-made Albany-Santiam Canal enters the Calapooia via a sizable waterfall. The Bryant Park boat ramp is about a hundred yards downstream on the left. In winter, don't venture out into the Willamette unless you are prepared to deal with a very strong current.

20

South Santiam River

Location: east of Albany
Distance: 20 miles
Time: 4 to 5 hours
USGS Maps: Lebanon, Crabtree, and Albany 7.5′
Best Season: all year
Rating: C

Boating on the South Santiam is usually associated with the whitewater sections of the upper river, where kayaks and rafts are essential equipment. The lower part of the river, however, while too tame for most whitewater enthusiasts, provides an excellent canoe trip in fast water. Although the lower river is not considered white water, its current is very strong and choppy sections are abundant. If you are looking for placid waters, this trip is not for you.

Start by leaving an extra car in Jefferson, a tiny town northeast of Albany. It can be reached from Interstate 5 by driving east from Exit 238 or 242 (see also the map for trip #21). Park your car near the public boat ramp at the foot of Ferry Street, a block north of the bridge, on the east bank of the river.

Then drive across the bridge and continue west from Jefferson about a mile. Turn left on Scravel Hill Road, and follow it to Highway 20. Turn left again, and follow Highway 20 into Lebanon. Turn left on Grant Street, following the signs to River Park. When you see the park and the bridge over the South Santiam, turn right, at a sign marked "Gill's Landing" to a large parking lot and a public boat ramp.

The river current is fast. In the first 10 miles, the channel drops almost 100 feet. This section has few landmarks other than islands and river bends; you probably will not be sure of your exact location until you reach Sanderson Bridge at Crabtree. If you are accustomed to paddling on slower waters, you will be amazed when you realize that you have just paddled 10 miles in much less than two hours.

Very little public land is located on this stretch of the river. A public boat ramp is located on the left bank, 0.4 miles past Sanderson Bridge, at the site of a former bridge.

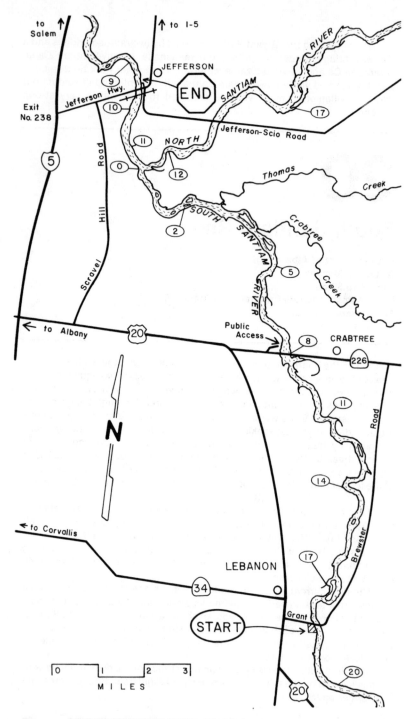

TRIP 20

On the South Santiam River

Winter is a good time to enjoy this river, if you dress properly and are lucky with the weather. Spring and late fall are also good, but in summer and early fall you will have to be very careful to avoid shallow sections.

The second 10 miles of this trip, from Sanderson Bridge to Jefferson, is similar to the first section, but a bit slower and smoother. Along the way, Crabtree Creek and Thomas Creek enter from the east, but they are both fairly small and you may miss them. The North Santiam, however, is hard to miss when it enters from the same direction. This junction is considered to be mile 0 of the South Santiam, but is mile 11.75 of the North Santiam and the main-branch Santiam River.

Just two miles downstream are the two railroad and highway bridges at Jefferson. The boat ramp is on the right bank, a few hundred feet past the bridges. If the current is strong, stay close to the right bank to make your landing.

21

Santiam River

Location: northeast of Albany
Distance: 11 miles
Time: 4 to 5 hours
USGS Maps: Albany, Sidney, Monmouth, and Lewisburg 7.5'
Best Season: all year
Rating: B

The Santiam River is not a typical Willamette River tributary. Unlike the motionless waters of the Luckiamute, the Yamhill, or the Pudding, the Santiam River is as big and as wide as the Willamette itself. This trip starts near the

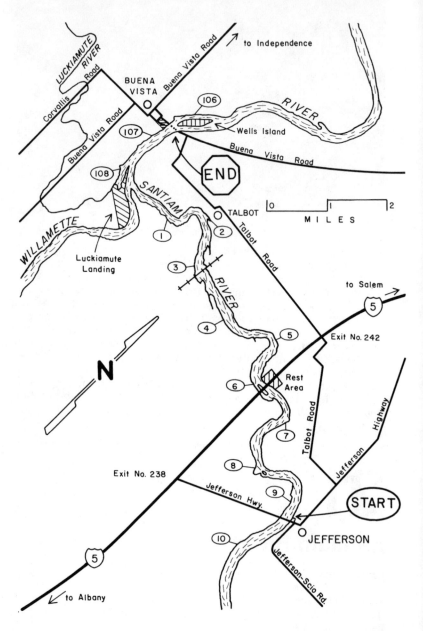

to Independence

BUENA VISTA

LUCKIAMUTE RIVER Road

Corvallis Road

Buena Vista Road

Buena Vista Road

106

RIVER

Wells Island

107

Buena Vista Road

108

END

SANTIAM

0   1   2
M I L E S

TALBOT

1

2

Talbot Road

Luckiamute Landing

WILLAMETTE

3

RIVER

to Salem

5

4

5

Exit No. 242

N

6

Rest Area

Talbot Road

Jefferson Highway

7

Exit No. 238

8

START

9

Jefferson Hwy.

JEFFERSON

5

10

Jefferson-Scio Rd.

to Albany

TRIP 21

Interstate 5 bridges across the Santiam River

confluence of the North Santiam and South Santiam rivers and travels down the main-branch Santiam River to the Willamette. An exploration of the quiet Luckiamute is an optional side trip.

The trip begins by leaving an extra car (or bicycle) at the Buena Vista Ferry. The ferry is reached from Interstate 5 via Talbot Road (Exit 242). Drive west through the small town of Talbot to the ferry landing a few miles beyond. Since the ferry does not run on weekends, you will probably park in a small parking area on the east bank, although a nice park and floating dock sit on the west bank.

Then drive east, back over the freeway, to the town of Jefferson. In the town, stay on the main street as it curves toward the river. Just before the bridge, turn right. At the foot of Ferry Street, a block north of the bridge, is a public boat ramp. But do not rush through Jefferson without at least looking around a little; some of the advantages of a town that has been bypassed by the freeway are obvious in Jefferson. A slow, small-town pace of life and more than a few architectural gems are just two of the benefits.

The Santiam is wide, with a moderately strong current. The island near mile 8 can be passed on either side, but the left channel seems the deepest. Just downstream is a feature aptly named "The Cliff."

Two miles downstream are the huge twin bridges of Interstate 5. A large rest area straddles the freeway here and gives access to a boat ramp on the north bank immediately downstream from the bridges. Due to the bridge piers and the strong current, non-motorized boats will have difficulty landing at the ramp. If you feel like stopping, land on the bank well upstream from the bridges.

The island under the south end of the bridges can be passed on either side, but the left channel is much rougher in winter, and much shallower in summer.

The Willamette Valley is home to numerous birds of prey. Watch for red-tailed hawks, kestrels, and the large marsh hawk with the telltale white patch on its rump. Ospreys can also be seen scouting the river for fish.

Large cliffs mark the junction of the Willamette from the south and the Luckiamute from the southwest. The Willamette seems smaller than the wide Santiam, and the Luckiamute is dwarfed by both. If you have some extra time, explore the mouth of the Luckiamute. Its quiet waters offer considerable contrast to the two torrents it joins. (See trip #22.)

From the mouth of the Luckiamute, the Buena Vista Ferry landing is just 1.5 miles downstream, near the head of Wells Island.

22

Luckiamute River

Location: north of Albany
Distance: 15 miles
Time: 5 to 6 hours
USGS Maps: Lewisburg and Monmouth 7.5'
Best Season: winter and spring
Rating: A

The Luckiamute River is a long meandering stream that begins in the Coast Range and wanders slowly eastward to join the Willamette River about eight miles north of Albany. Its name (pronounced "Luckymute") is Indian in origin, but its meaning is not known.

Winter and spring are the best seasons to visit the Luckiamute. During much of the year, the river is slow and narrow. Its numerous snags collect debris and create small logjams. When the winter rains arrive, however, the current strengthens, the water level rises, and the river is usually cleared out, providing a fairly fast and uninterrupted trip for canoeists.

The 15-mile trip described below can be paddled in about five or six hours on a strong winter/spring current. The trip will take much longer in the summer; either get an early start, or shorten the trip by beginning or ending at Davidson Bridge, located at mile 6.

Start the trip by leaving an extra car or bicycle at Buena Vista Park, a county park located in the small town of Buena Vista. The town can be

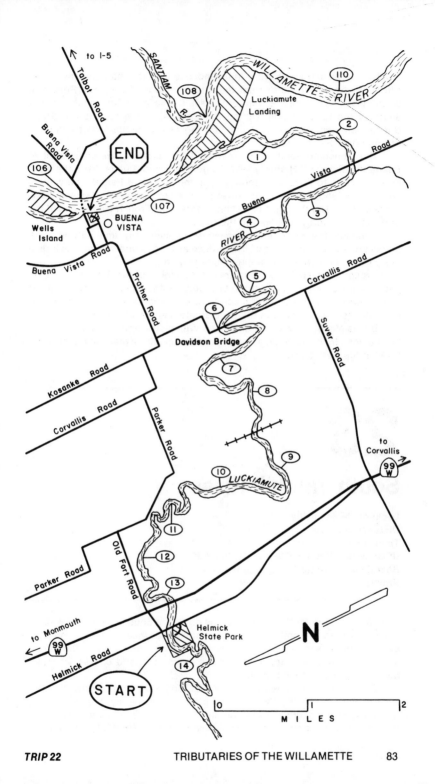

reached by driving south from Independence (see the map accompanying trip #6) or by driving north from the Albany area on Spring Hill Road and Buena Vista Road (see the map for trip #5). Buena Vista Park is located just south of the ferry landing. During the week when the ferry is operating, Buena Vista can also be reached by driving west from the Talbot Road exit off Interstate 5 (Exit 242).

The launching point, Helmick State Park, is about five miles west of Buena Vista, just off Highway 99W. To get there from Buena Vista, the most direct route is to drive west through the community of Parker; you will encounter two short sections of gravel road. When you reach Highway 99W, cross it and follow the signs to Helmick State Park. From the north end of the park, several short paths lead to the river.

Although the Luckiamute meanders considerably and natural landmarks are few, the presence of five bridges at various intervals makes it relatively easy to determine an approximate location.

Except for the public access area at the mouth of the river, there are no public lands on this section of the Luckiamute. The bay at the mouth of the river, however, is an excellent place to stop. Paddle around the bay, or explore the peninsula between the Luckiamute and the Willamette.

Buena Vista is 1.5 miles down the Willamette from the mouth of the Luckiamute. In the summer, a floating dock is usually in place at Buena Vista Park on the west bank.

23

South Yamhill River

Location: McMinnville
Distance: 9 miles
Time: 4 hours
USGS Maps: McMinnville and Dayton 7.5′
Best Season: winter through midsummer
Rating: A

This tour starts in McMinnville, paddles down the South Yamhill River to its junction with the Yamhill, and then continues three miles farther to the town of Lafayette. In winter and spring, these two rivers are slow and flat, but in summer a few minor rapids will require some care, and one set of major rapids will require a short portage.

Start by leaving an extra car at C. E. Terry Park in Lafayette, 35 miles west of Portland on Highway 99W. The park is on the south side of town, where Highway 233 crosses the Yamhill. This park was once the town's central square, but the center of town shifted to Highway 99W after steamboat

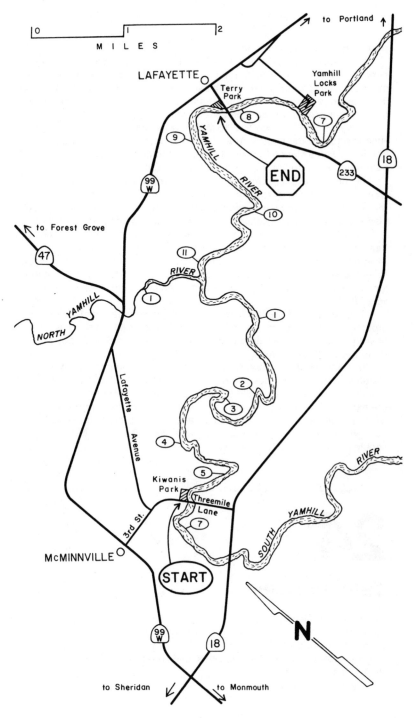

traffic on the river diminished.

Before leaving this park, take a look at the river just upstream from the park. In summer, a large set of rapids will be readily apparent (or audible), requiring a short portage on the north bank. In winter and spring, these rapids (and the ledge on the north bank used for the portage) will be under several feet of flat water and should present no obstacle.

Drive west on Highway 99W to McMinnville, and follow the signs toward Highway 18 and the airport. After 3rd Street becomes Threemile Lane, turn left into Kiwanis Marine Park just before the bridge over the South Yamhill. A boat ramp is located on the loop road through the park.

In summer, expect some minor rapids at the sharp bend near mile 5, and watch for two more in the bends just before mile 4. In winter and spring, these rapids will not be present, but when the water drops in summer, exercise some care. By late summer, these rapids will usually be quite shallow.

The river miles shown on the sketch map may be a bit confusing. The Yamhill, the South Yamhill, and the North Yamhill are considered to be separate rivers, and their miles are usually numbered separately. An interesting side trip would be to paddle up the North Yamhill, but it is even smaller than the South Yamhill. In summer, do not count on being able to go very far.

The last part of the trip is tricky during the summer months. When approaching Lafayette, stay near the left bank, and head for shore when you hear the rapids. Take advantage of the portage around these rapids; do not try to paddle through them.

Immediately after the rapids is Terry Park and time to exit. You could continue another mile downstream to Yamhill Locks Park (the launching point for trip #24), but a couple of small rapids are in between, and access to the park from above the old locks is difficult at best. During periods of high water (winter and spring), the rapids and the falls next to the locks are flooded, and an easy landing can be made below the locks, but this option should be checked out in advance.

24

Yamhill River

Location: near Newberg
Distance: 12 miles
Time: 4 to 5 hours
USGS Maps: Dayton, St. Paul, Dundee, and Newberg 7.5′
NOAA Chart: #18528
Best Season: all year
Rating: A

A two-person touring kayak at Yamhill Locks Park

It is difficult to believe that large steamboats once cruised the lazy waters of the Yamhill River, but a huge set of locks were built for their use just outside the town of Lafayette. This trip begins at the locks, travels seven miles down the Yamhill to the Willamette, then goes five miles farther on the Willamette to Newberg.

Begin by leaving a car at the public boat ramp in Newberg, at the foot of River Street. (When entering Newberg from Portland, turn left on River Street, just past Herbert Hoover Park.) Then drive southwest on Highway 99W toward Lafayette. Look for a left turn marked "Yamhill Locks Park," and follow it to the park. If you reach Lafayette, you have driven too far on Highway 99W.

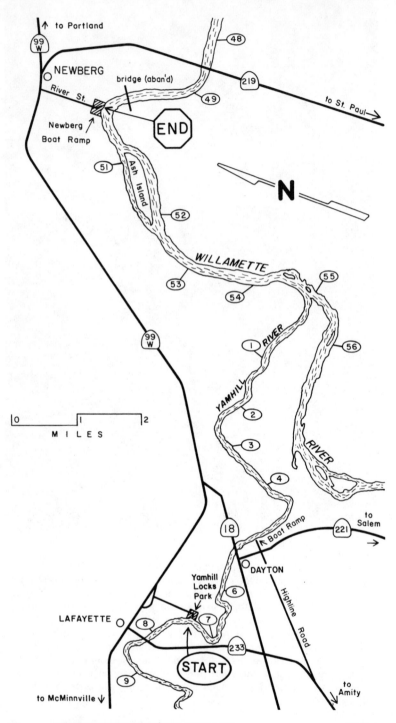

The locks, some 275 feet long, were built between 1897 and 1900, along with a 16-foot dam, to facilitate boat traffic up the Yamhill to McMinnville. Today the dam is gone, but the locks still stand next to the rapids known as Yamhill Falls. In winter and spring, the falls will be under several feet of smooth water.

Launch your boat below the falls. The trip downstream is smooth and lazy. You might see a few fishermen with outboards, but not enough to really disturb this tranquil river. At Dayton, the river crosses under Highway 18 and then passes a public boat ramp that could be used as a starting or ending point for a shorter trip.

The Yamhill has little current to it, so you will be glad when it joins the faster Willamette. From the mouth of the Yamhill, Newberg is five miles downstream. Watch for red-tailed hawks and great blue herons. Also watch for the ski boats that will not be watching for you.

Two miles from Newberg, look for a row of pilings on the left bank, indicating the entrance to the slough behind Ash Island. The slough has less current than the main channel of the river, but also a lot fewer motorboats, so it is a wise choice.

The island is private property (as evidenced by the private ferry used to cross the main channel). The Newberg boat ramp is just a mile downstream from Ash Island.

25

Pudding River

Location: Aurora/Canby area
Distance: 9 miles
Time: 4 hours
USGS Maps: Yoder, Woodburn, and Canby 7.5'
NOAA Chart: #18528
Best Season: winter and spring
Rating: A

The Pudding River has its origins in the foothills east of Salem, but it flows north to join the Molalla and Willamette rivers near Canby. Its name originates from pioneer days when a group of tired and wet settlers prepared elk blood pudding on its banks.

The trip begins by leaving an extra car at the Molalla River State Park on the south side of the Willamette River, a half mile west of the Canby Ferry.

The put-in spot is northeast of Aurora. A few hundred feet northeast of the Highway 99E bridge over the Pudding, turn north on a gravel road and drive 0.25 miles to a railroad bridge. Limited parking is available on the shoulder.

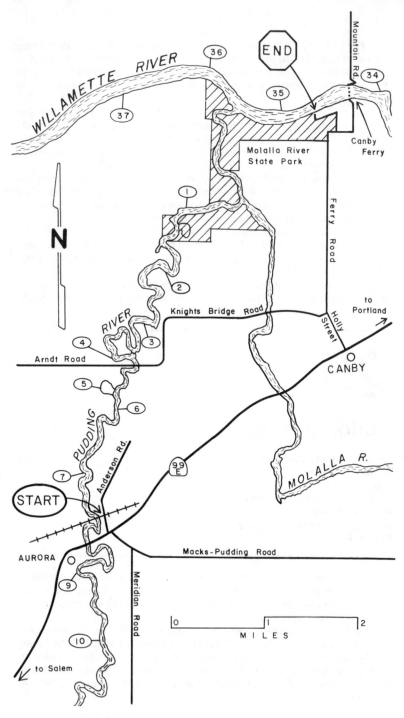

TRIBUTARIES OF THE WILLAMETTE   *TRIP 25*

Unless the river has been doing some major excavation work on its banks, the trip should be fairly uneventful. Watch for beaver and muskrat and birds such as kingfishers and green herons. Slackwater pools off to the sides indicate former oxbows abandoned by a river that could not make up its mind. Because of frequent changes in the channel, the river miles marked on USGS maps (and the sketch map printed here) are not particularly accurate.

Immediately north of the Arndt Road Bridge (mile 4.5) the river demonstrates its indecisiveness. In 1980 it broke through a large oxbow and occupied two separate channels around the resulting island. The right channel was faster and shorter, while the left was more leisurely; but in 1981 the property owner built a causeway to his newly created island. As a result, the river has returned to its original channel to the west.

Eventually the muddy waters of the Pudding join the relatively clear waters of the Molalla (see trip #26) and a mile later reaches the Willamette. A major heron rookery is located on the right bank in the cottonwood trees along this mile of the Molalla. In the winter, when the leaves are off the trees, the nests are clearly visible. In the summer, look for the euphemistic "whitewash."

Turn right on the Willamette, and watch for the small state park boat ramp on the right bank about a half mile downstream. Also keep a careful eye on the powerboats that swarm the area.

26

Molalla River

Location: near Canby
Distance: 5 or 16 miles
Time: 3 or 6 hours
USGS Maps: Molalla, Yoder, and Canby 7.5'
Best Season: spring
Rating: A or C

The Molalla River is a long river that drains much of western Clackamas County. Through most of its journey, it is a steep mountain stream, a fact belied by the calm waters that pass through the farm country near Canby.

The 16-mile trip described here offers samples of both parts of the river. The first 11 miles drop about 150 feet in elevation and offer the experienced paddler numerous opportunities to get wet. The inexperienced paddler, who is more likely to take advantage of those opportunities, should limit the trip to the last 5 miles by launching in Canby. Some of the more experienced paddlers, on the other hand, might want to end their trip in Canby, if flatwater paddling puts them to sleep.

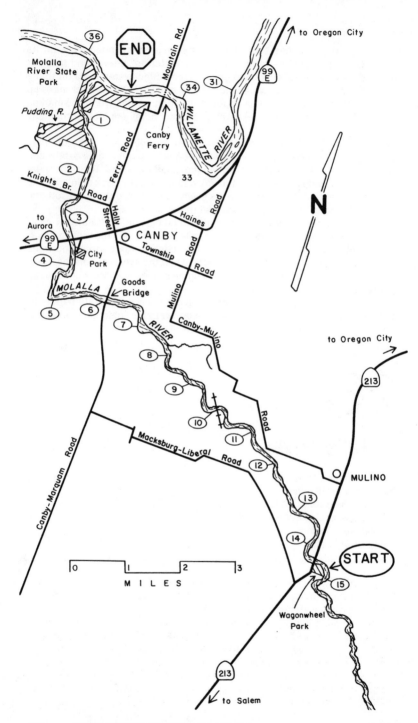

The trip begins by leaving an extra car near Canby, either at the Molalla River State Park north of town or at a city park just west of town. To reach the state park from Canby, drive north on Holly Street and Ferry Road. The city park can be reached from Canby by driving west on Highway 99E. Just before the highway crosses the river, turn left on Berg Parkway and follow it a quarter mile to the park. Inexperienced paddlers will want to begin their trip at this city park. Alternate launching areas are available at Goods Bridge (mile 6) or at Knights Bridge (mile 2.5).

For the rest of you, the launching point is Wagonwheel County Park. From Canby, drive east on Canby-Mulino Road. In Mulino, turn right on Highway 213, and follow it to Wagonwheel Park, located on the east side of the highway just after crossing the river.

Immediately past the launching site, the river will be moderately rough, with a few small waves and countless gravel bars and shallow spots. Watch the channel carefully, and try to stay in the deepest water. In one or two places a short portage across a gravel bar should be considered to avoid having to wade to shore. By the time the river reaches Goods Bridge at mile 6, the river will have spent itself, and you can spend more of your time watching the scenery rather than the river.

Although those who prefer to let the current do the work might omit the last few miles by landing at Canby, they will miss a very scenic section of the river. The Pudding joins from the west near mile 1, and the newly strengthened river glides past a large heron rookery on the east bank. After turning east on the Willamette, the state park boat ramp is just a half mile downstream.

27

Tualatin River—Scholls to Schamberg Bridge

Location: Scholls area, Washington County
Distance: 11 miles
Time: 6 hours
USGS Maps: Scholls and Beaverton 7.5'
Best Season: all year
Rating: A

The section of the Tualatin River east of Scholls is the most circuitous portion of the river. As the crow flies, Schamberg Bridge is only 4 miles from Scholls, but the river spends 11 lazy miles covering it. Since the Tualatin has little or no current, this fairly long trip deserves an early start.

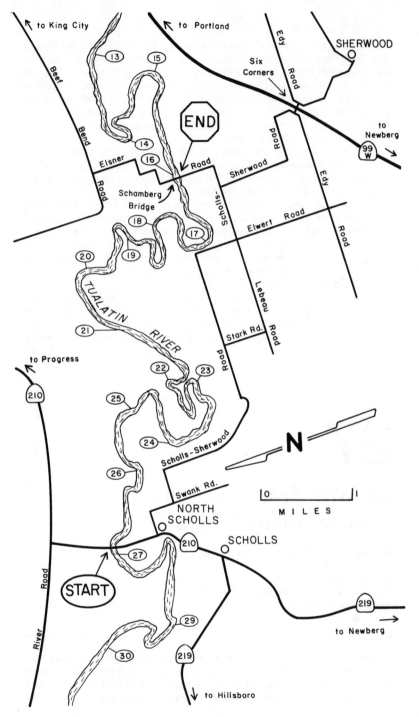

TRIBUTARIES OF THE WILLAMETTE *TRIP 27*

Kayaks on the Tualatin River

Begin by leaving an extra car (or a bicycle) at Schamberg Bridge. From Portland, drive south on Highway 99W 4.1 miles past King City to Six Corners. Turn right and drive north toward Scholls on Scholls-Sherwood Road. Follow it as it turns west then north again. Turn right on Elsner Road, and drive 0.75 miles to the bridge. Limited parking is available on the shoulder.

The put-in point is reached by returning to Scholls-Sherwood Road and continuing west, then north and west to the tiny community of North Scholls. Turn right (north) and drive a half mile to the bridge. A short path at the northeast end of the bridge gives access to the river.

The bridge is a fairly new one; remains of a predecessor can be seen beneath it. Scholls Ferry, named for a pioneer who first settled in the area in 1847, operated at this site for many years.

The river in this area is devoid of landmarks; you will have a difficult time determining exactly how far you have traveled. A compass and copies of the two topographic maps will be very helpful if you would like to know exactly where you are. A watch and a rough idea of your average speed also help, but it is still a difficult task.

The meandering section of the river between miles 21 and 25 was known by early steamboat crews as either the Seven Bends or the Grecian Bend. History has it that the crews of different boats could converse across the narrow isthmuses as the boats plied the river.

The destination, Schamberg Bridge, is near mile 16. The best access to the road is on the right bank immediately east of the bridge.

Crawfish trapping on the Tualatin River

28

Tualatin River—Schamberg Bridge to Lake Oswego

Location: near Tualatin
Distance: 11 miles
Time: 5 hours
USGS Maps: Beaverton and Lake Oswego 7.5′
Best Season: all year
Rating: A

This trip covers the 11-mile section of the Tualatin River from Schamberg Bridge, near Sherwood, to Shipley Bridge, near Lake Oswego. Although the entire 16 miles from Schamberg Bridge to the Willamette River are navigable, the last 5 miles should be avoided by ending the trip at Shipley Bridge. These last miles involve a portage around a small dam, some shallow rocky stretches during low water, and some rough and dangerous stretches during high water.

Begin this trip by leaving your extra car or bicycle near Shipley Bridge on Stafford Road near Wankers Corner. Just north of the bridge, turn east on Shadow Wood Drive and follow it a quarter mile to a small landing.

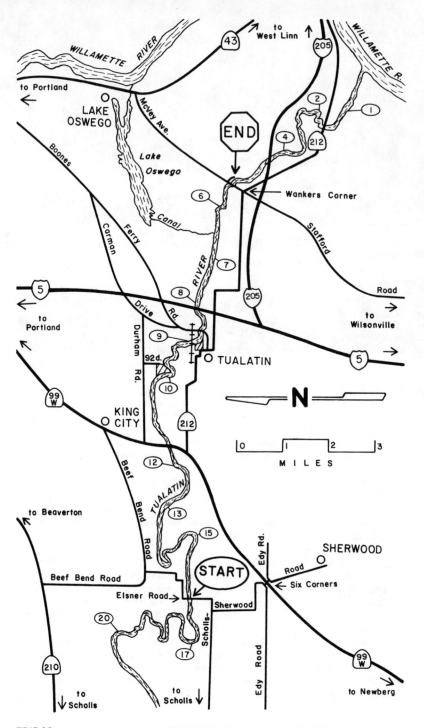

On the Tualatin River

To reach the starting point, Schamberg Bridge, from Wankers Corner, drive west on Highway 212 through Tualatin to Highway 99W. Turn left and drive 2.7 miles to Six Corners. Turn right there, and drive north toward Scholls on Scholls-Sherwood Road as it turns west and north again. Turn right on Elsner Road, and drive 0.75 miles to the bridge. Parking space is fairly limited. The best access to the river is via a small ravine at the southeast end of the bridge.

If you do not feel like paddling a full 11 miles of river with no current to speak of, you might consider starting your trip near Tualatin at either of two city parks shown on the sketch map.

At mile 11.5, the river passes under Highway 99W. Taylors Ferry was operated at this site for many years, and during the 1920's the crossing was served by a huge covered bridge.

The city parks are located at miles 9 and 10, complete with boat ramps and picnic facilities. Unfortunately, this section of the river is presently under consideration for "improvement," including dredging, dikes, and overflow channels to protect buildings unwisely located in the river's flood plain.

At mile 6.5, watch for an opening in the underbrush on the left bank for a "canal" to Lake Oswego. This canal was hand-dug in the 1870's to allow steamboats to bypass the unnavigable lower portion of the Tualatin. Included in the same scheme were plans for locks at the lower end of the lake, to allow water traffic from Portland to Hillsboro without interruption. Although the locks were never built, steamboats used the canal for several years. Today, overgrown and unnavigable, its only purpose is to maintain the water level of Lake Oswego.

COLUMBIA RIVER

29

Lacamas Creek and Lake

Location: north of Camas, Washington
Distance: 4 miles
Time: 4 hours
USGS Maps: Lacamas Creek and Camas 7.5' or Camas 15'
Best Season: all year
Rating: B

Lacamas Creek is a pretty stream that drains much of the farmland east of Vancouver. About a mile north of Camas, Lacamas Lake was formed when a dam was built, backing the stream's water up for about three miles. The trip described here begins about a mile upstream from the lake, where the river begins to lose its strong current. After entering the lake, the trip paddles the length of the lake to a county park near the dam.

Begin the trip by leaving an extra car or bicycle at Clark County's Lacamas Lake Park. From Vancouver, the park can be reached by driving east on Highway 14 about 13 miles to the Camas exit. In downtown Camas, drive east on 3rd Street, then turn left onto Garfield Street (Highway 500). About a mile north of town, the park is located on the right, just before the bridge between Round Lake and Lacamas Lake.

The launching point is reached by continuing north on Highway 500, then following Leadbetter Road, as shown on the sketch map, towards the bridge on Goodwin Road. Immediately after crossing the bridge, park on the left.

Lacamas Creek is fairly swift and shallow as it passes under the bridge. Downstream and within sight from the bridge, the current slows considerably, becoming quite placid.

If the stream is not navigable due to low water, the trip can be salvaged by launching along Leadbetter Road. If you do launch on the lake, be sure to paddle back up into the mouth of Lacamas Creek, since the transition zone between the fast water of the stream and the still water of the lake is the prettiest part of this trip. The narrow channel, which broadens as it approaches the lake, presents numerous opportunities to linger. The bird population is particularly diverse. Geese, ducks, hawks, and numerous songbirds can be expected to make appearances.

The lake itself is long and open. Watch the southern horizon for glimpses of Mt. Hood. In windy weather, try to stay close to the shore for both shelter and safety.

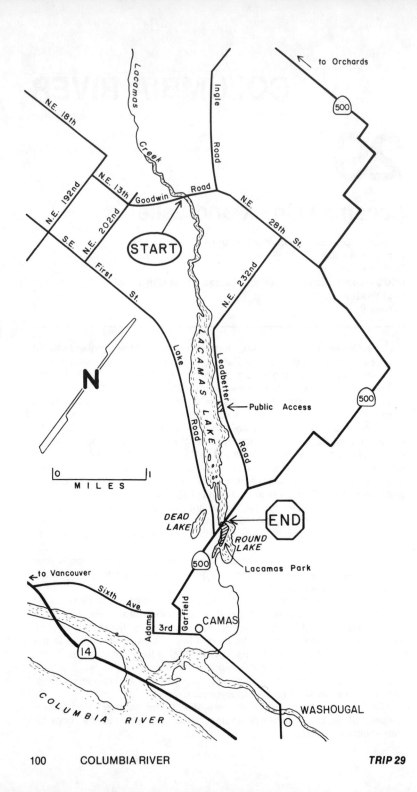

Lacamas Creek

The southern end of the lake presents a half-dozen islands for exploring, lunching, or napping, before returning to your car near the Highway 500 bridge.

30

Columbia Slough

Location: north Portland
Distance: variable
Time: 2 to 6 hours
USGS Maps: Sauvie Island, Linnton, and Portland 7.5′
NOAA Charts: #18526 or #18524
Best Season: all year
Rating: A

The Columbia Slough is a narrow backwater channel that runs from the Columbia River near N.E. 33rd Drive to the Willamette near Kelley Point Park. Parts of it are less than scenic, but other parts offer relative seclusion despite nearby industrial activity. Spring is a particularly good time to visit

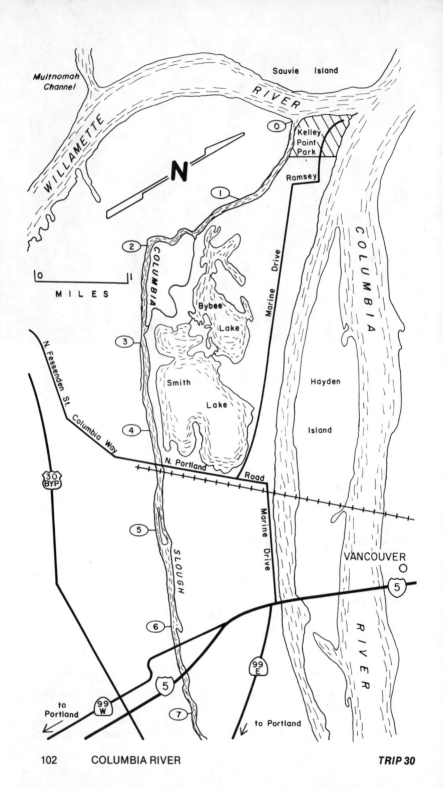

Multnomah Channel

Sauvie Island

RIVER

WILLAMETTE

N

Kelley Point Park

Ramsey

Marine Drive

COLUMBIA

COLUMBIA

Bybee Lake

Smith Lake

Hayden Island

N. Fessenden St.

Columbia Way

N. Portland Road

Marine Drive

SLOUGH

VANCOUVER

to Portland

to Portland

RIVER

0 — 1

M I L E S

30 BYP

99 W

99 E

5

5

5

the slough, when wildlife activity is at a peak. Take your bird book and a pair of binoculars, and watch for herons and various hawks; or take a pole and angle for panfish.

Access to the slough is not very good. For much of its length, particularly along its eastern end, no public access is available, and attempts to launch a canoe will bring a rapid response from various security guards. Even portions of Delta Park that border the slough are often closed to the public.

Two possible access points will be described here. The first is Kelley Point Park, at the confluence of the two rivers. It is a beautiful park, with pleasant woods and sandy beaches, but the beach is a hundred-yard portage from the parking lot. To reach the slough from Kelley Point, paddle west on the Columbia around the jetty on the point, then up the Willamette about a half mile. Just before the huge grain elevator, turn left to find the mouth of the slough. (While on the Columbia and Willamette, be careful of the wakes caused by huge commercial ships.)

A second access point is located where the slough is crossed by North Portland Road. Park on the north side of the slough, between the road and the railroad. A short dirt road leads down to the water.

These points are about five miles apart. A one-way paddle could be arranged between them, or to avoid the inconvenience of a car shuttle, launch at one or the other and make a round-trip paddle up the slough and back again. In planning your trip, consult the tide tables to determine the direction of the gentle tidal current.

Also take a glance at a current weather forecast. Kelley Point Park is a favorite of kite fliers, with good reason. Plan ahead, and don't end up paddling back to your car while fighting both the tide and the wind.

31

Sauvie Island

Location: 12 miles north of Portland
Distance: variable
Time: 1 to 6 hours
USGS Maps: Sauvie Island and St. Helens 7.5′
NOAA Chart: #18524
Best Season: winter through early fall
Rating: A

Sauvie (not Sauvies) Island is said to be the largest freshwater island in the country. Much of it is covered by myriad lakes and sloughs, offering endless opportunities for flatwater paddling.

Sandhill cranes

The island has a long history, from early Indian settlements to a visit by Lewis and Clark in 1805. First settled by white men in the 1830's, it was named for a French-Canadian employee of the Hudson's Bay Company dairy that was once operated on the island.

Nearly all of the wetlands on the island are closed to the non-hunting public during the fall duck hunting season, which usually runs from mid-October to mid-January. Call the area manager at (503) 621-3488 or the Oregon Wildlife Commission at (503) 229-5403 for current information on closures and hunting.

To get to Sauvie Island from Portland, drive north on Highway 30 about 12 miles to the Sauvie Island Bridge. Cross the bridge and drive north past the store on Gilliham Loop Road.

The launching point for your canoe depends on the season and on which portions of the island you want to explore. Three possibilities will be described here; others can be seen on the sketch map, or by stopping at the game refuge headquarters on Sauvie Island Road just north of Reeder Road and picking up a copy of their more detailed map. Wildlife watchers should also pick up a copy of their bird and animal checklist.

Oak Island is a good place to launch for quick access to the main part of Sturgeon Lake. The island (actually a peninsula) can be reached by driving northeast on Reeder Road and turning left on Oak Island Road (see map for trip #32). A small fee is usually charged to use the Oak Island area.

The main part of Sturgeon Lake can also be reached by boat from Coon Point Access, except in late summer or early fall when the Coon Point area is dry. To reach the access area, drive northeast on Reeder Road to a small roadside parking area, then carry your boat over the dike. Paddle northeast, then northwest to get to the main portion of the lake.

The third choice for launching is at the north end of Reeder Road. After Reeder Road turns to gravel, follow it for another mile to a left turn, which leads to the Gilbert River boat ramp. Just before you reach the boat ramp, the road passes the shore of one of the numerous lakes north of Sturgeon Lake. Paddle south through these lakes and their interconnecting sloughs as far as time and water levels permit. A few floating footbridges will require short portages. If you paddle as far south as Sturgeon Lake, the return trip to

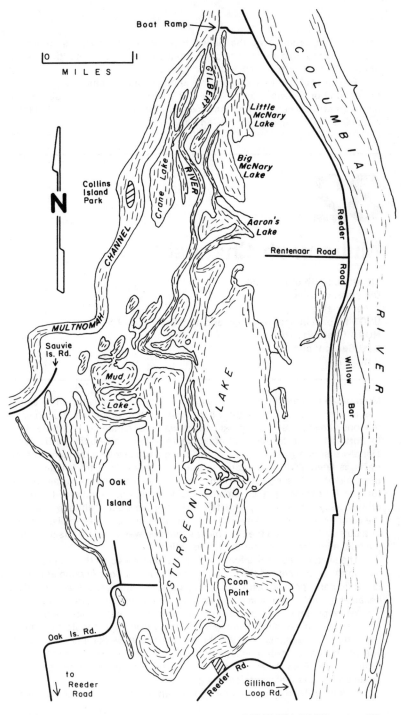

Boat Ramp

0   MILES   1

N

COLUMBIA

Collins Island Park

Little McNary Lake

Big McNary Lake

Aaron's Lake

Reeder Road

Rentenaar Road

CRANE LAKE

GILBERT RIVER

MULTNOMAH CHANNEL

Sauvie Is. Rd.

Mud Lake

STURGEON LAKE

Willow Bar

RIVER

Oak Island

Coon Point

Oak Is. Rd.

to Reeder Road

Reeder Rd.

Gillihan Loop Rd.

your car can be made via the Gilbert River. Although "river" is not an accurate name for this muddy slough, it connects Sturgeon Lake with the Multnomah Channel to the northwest (see trip #32).

Even if you've left your binoculars at home, opportunities for birdwatching abound on Sauvie Island. Some of the larger, more obvious species include great blue herons, whistling swans, Canada geese, sandhill cranes, red-tailed hawks, turkey vultures, and marsh hawks.

32

Multnomah Channel

Location: north of Portland
Distance: variable
Time: variable
USGS Maps: Linnton, Sauvie Island, and St. Helens 7.5′
NOAA Chart: #18524
Best Season: all year
Rating: A

Multnomah Channel forms the western shore of Sauvie Island, which sits in the mouth of the Willamette where it joins the Columbia. For several reasons, the channel is a popular body of water for canoeing. It is quite close to Portland, yet offers a rural atmosphere. While powerboat traffic occasionally disrupts the tranquility of the slough, the size and frequency of the traffic is limited when compared to the main channels of the Willamette or the Columbia. The slough's 21 miles of length offer considerable opportunities for exploring, and numerous boat ramps and commercial marinas provide easy access to any selected portion of the slough, although some of the commercial operators may charge a small launching fee. Finally, the lack of a current (other than the tide) means that two-way trips are easily accomplished, eliminating any car shuttle logistics.

The sketch map shows four public boat ramps, two on the mainland and two on the island side of the channel. The Columbia County ramp at mile 12 is particularly popular with beginning paddlers and groups of canoeists because an adjacent commercial marina has canoes available for rent.

When planning your trip, be conservative in estimating how many miles you will want to paddle. It is unlikely that you will want to paddle much more than 10 or 12 miles, especially if the wind or tide is working against you. If you would like to cover much more than that, consider an overnight visit to Collins Island Park (shown on some maps as Coon Island), one of the few areas on the channel where camping is permitted.

If you get tired of paddling up and down the channel, several adjacent

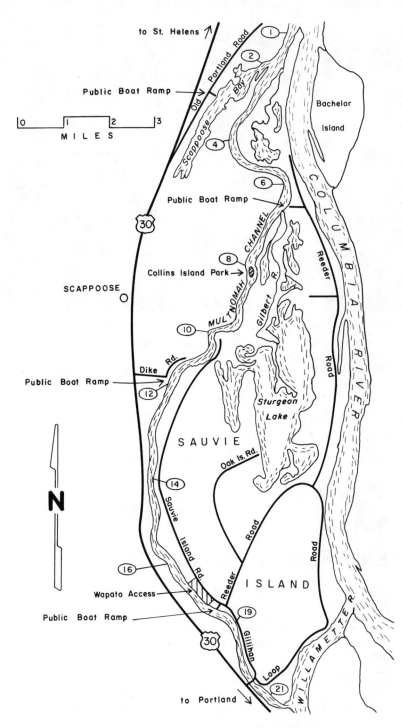

to St. Helens

Portland Road

Public Boat Ramp

Old Scappoose Bay

①
②
④
⑥

Public Boat Ramp

CHANNEL

Bachelor Island

COLUMBIA RIVER

Reeder

⑧ Collins Island Park

MULTNOMAH

Gilbert R.

⑩

SCAPPOOSE ○

Dike Rd.

Public Boat Ramp

⑫

Road

Sturgeon Lake

SAUVIE

Oak Is. Rd.

⑭

Sauvie Island Rd.

N

⑯

Reeder Road

Road

ISLAND

Wapato Access

Public Boat Ramp

⑲

Gillihan

30

WILLAMETTE R.

Loop

⑳①

to Portland

MILES

0   1   2   3

Houseboats along the Multnomah Channel

areas are worth exploring. Scappoose Bay is large and intricate, but also extremely shallow at low tide.

Sauvie Island offers three sloughs that can be entered from Multnomah Channel. At the north end of the island, Cunningham Slough leads to Cunningham Lake. Near the narrow portion of the island, two sloughs enter the island. The southernmost leads to Crane Lake, and the northern of the two (the Gilbert River) travels about five miles into the interior of the island to Sturgeon Lake. A more detailed map of the Sturgeon Lake area accompanies trip #31.

33

East Fork of the Lewis River

Location: 25 miles north of Portland
Distance: 9.5 miles
Time: 4 to 5 hours
USGS Maps: Battleground and Ridgefield 7.5′
Best Season: winter through early spring
Rating: C

The East Fork of the Lewis River is misnamed: it is south, not east, of the main branch of the river, and is large enough to warrant a separate name. Its upper stretches are clear and very swift, while the last few miles are tidal. The portion described here covers the transition zone between mountain stream and coastal river. The first few miles are choppy and not for the inexperienced, while the lower miles, as the river passes through expansive pasturelands, require steady paddling on flat water.

Begin the trip by leaving your extra car at Paradise Point State Park, 25 miles north of Portland on Interstate 5. The boat ramp is directly under the freeway bridges. As you enter the park, keep to the left away from the campground to reach the ramp area.

The launching point is reached by driving south and east via the route shown on the sketch map. When you reach the entrance to Daybreak State Park, turn left and drive to the end of a short dead-end road west of the bridge. The river is quite rough as it passes under this bridge, so most boaters prefer to launch below the bridge rather than at Daybreak Park just upstream.

Before you launch, look closely at the river and the rapids under the bridge. If the rapids look difficult to you, you had best launch farther downstream, since the three or four miles immediately below this bridge involve several similar rapids. Alternate launching points are available near mile 7.5 and mile 3, as shown on the sketch map.

None of the rapids are particularly difficult, but all will require quick choices between channels and a few possible quick turns. The river channel has undergone considerable change recently and will no doubt continue to do so; be careful, particularly in cold weather or when paddling down blind channels. In 1981, a large group of islands near mile 8 were best passed via the northernmost channel.

Bridge at La Center

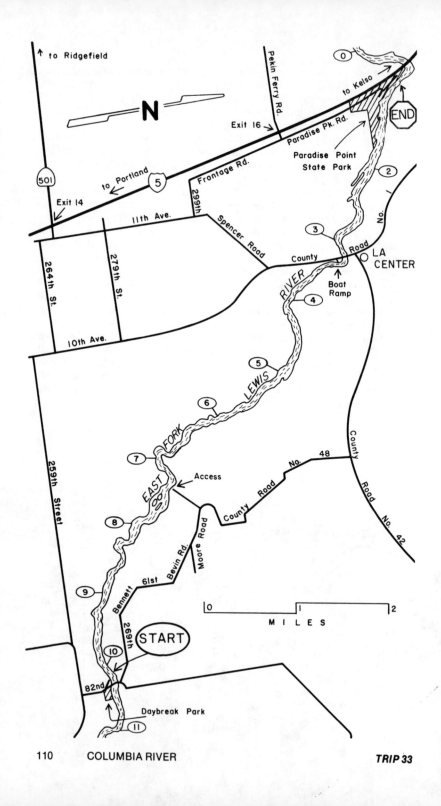

A large power line appears overhead at mile 7.25, marking a popular fishing area. Shortly afterward, the river valley widens considerably. Dikes and broad pastures dominate the scene, particularly in the winter when both are occasionally under several feet of water.

The town of La Center, near mile 3, is marked by a distinctive arched bridge. Paradise Point is about two miles downstream, but the time taken to paddle this section will depend partly on whether the tide is coming in or going out.

34

Lewis River

Location: Woodland, Washington
Distance: 9 miles
Time: 4 to 5 hours
USGS Maps: Ariel and Woodland 7.5′
Best Season: winter through early spring
Rating: B

The Lewis River is a southwest Washington river that enters the Columbia near the Oregon town of St. Helens. The trip described here, however, ends a few miles up the river at the town of Woodland.

To start this trip, drive north from Vancouver on Interstate 5 about 21 miles to the town of Woodland (Exit 21). Just east of the freeway interchange, cross the river via a bridge, and leave your extra car or bicycle at the gravel boat ramp and parking area on the north side of the bridge. While you are there, look upstream about half a mile to the small waterfall that blocks the river. The size of these falls fluctuates with the tide, but will usually require a short portage.

Then cross back over the bridge and drive north and east on Highway 503, following the signs towards Merwin Dam. About seven miles from Woodland, turn right at signs marking a Washington state fish hatchery. After stopping for a few minutes to watch the thousands of immature salmon, drive through the hatchery and turn right on a small gravel road just past the last pond. Launch your boat from the large gravel area below the ponds.

The upper half of this trip travels through steep wooded territory. The current is fairly strong, but little rough water is encountered. Between miles 14 and 15, several small islands require careful choices to avoid shallow water.

Past mile 12, the head of a huge island appears. Although a public fishing and launching area is located a short distance down the right-hand

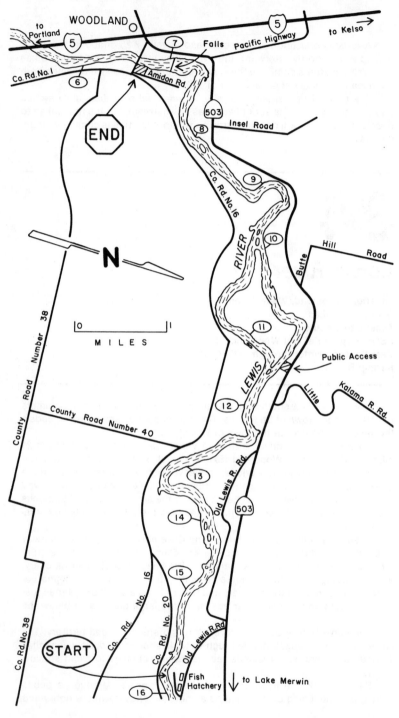

channel, the main channel continues to the left and is the best course to follow past this two-mile-long island.

The character of the river begins to change slightly as it passes the island. Like a coastal river approaching the ocean, the banks become sandy in places and are populated by beach grasses and Scotch broom. On a warm day, find a sand bar for a lunch break or an afternoon nap.

As you approach the town of Woodland, the number of vacation homes and mobile homes increases, disturbing the wilderness quality of the river. As you enter the town, look and listen for the falls at mile 7. Almost invariably, these falls require a portage, usually on the left bank. Occasionally high tide or high runoff may make them navigable, but at least scout them from shore prior to attempting to paddle them.

The Woodland bridge and the end of this trip are about half a mile downstream from the falls.

35

Tenasillahe Island

Location: near Cathlamet
Distance: 2 to 5 miles
Time: 3 to 6 hours
USGS Maps: Cathlamet and Skamokawa 15′
NOAA Chart: #18523
Best Season: all year
Rating: A

In the Columbia River, about 20 miles east of Astoria, several islands and part of the Washington mainland have been set aside as a refuge for a subspecies of deer that lives only along the lower Columbia River. Tenasillahe Island is the largest of the islands that make up this Columbian White-tailed Deer National Wildlife Refuge. In addition to wildlife watching, the refuge offers pleasant canoeing on both quiet backwater sloughs and the open waters of the main channel of the Columbia.

The best launching spot is on the Washington shore, on Steamboat Slough Road. To get there, drive about 2 miles west and north on Highway 4 from Cathlamet, Washington. Just after crossing the Elochoman River bridge, turn left on Steamboat Slough Road. Drive 2.6 miles to a small beach on the Columbia near navigational marker #37.

The quickest way to drive to Cathlamet from Portland is to drive north on I-5 to Kelso, then drive west on Highway 4; but a more leisurely and scenic route utilizes the Wahkiakum County Ferry to Puget Island. From Portland,

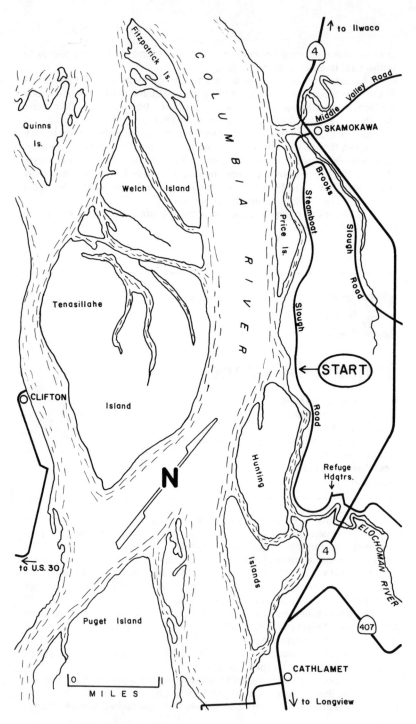

drive north on Highway 30 (St. Helens Road) to Westport, where the ferry departs for Puget Island hourly on the half hour. The ferry ride is definitely worth the small toll and delivers you to within a few miles of Cathlamet.

Launching from the Washington shore has one drawback: Tenasillahe Island is across the main Columbia River shipping lane. The island is less than a mile away, but the cautious paddler would be wise not to start the crossing in foggy weather or if any ships are visible in either direction. Alternate launching spots are at Aldrich Point (see trip #36) or at Clifton (turn right on Clifton Road about six miles west of Westport on U.S. 30), but both would involve a longer paddle to the destination, the slough between Tenasillahe Island and Welch Island.

A levee has been built around the perimeter of Tenasillahe Island to keep it from being inundated at high water. Floodgates at the back of a small bay on the northwest corner of the island allow the water to flow out of the island's internal sloughs, but prevent it from entering the island during periods of high water.

The sloughs of Tenasillahe Island and nearby Welch Island offer excellent birdwatching. Watch for several species of herons, gulls, ducks, and hawks. In winter, be on the lookout for bald eagles. Also keep an eye on the direction of the tide, so you will know whether your trip back to your car will be with or against it.

Although hunting is not currently allowed on Tenasillahe Island, the refuge does permit hunting along portions of the Washington shore during fall duck hunting season. If you plan on exploring the islands and sloughs on the Washington side of the river in the fall, you should visit the refuge headquarters or call them at (206) 795-4915 to determine when and where hunting is allowed.

36

Aldrich Point

Location: east of Astoria
Distance: variable
Time: about 5 hours
USGS Maps: Svenson and Grays River 15′
NOAA Chart: #18523
Best Season: all year
Rating: A

Lewis and Clark National Wildlife Refuge includes dozens of islands in the Columbia River between Astoria and Aldrich Point, 15 miles to the east. The refuge offers both open waters and narrow backwater sloughs.

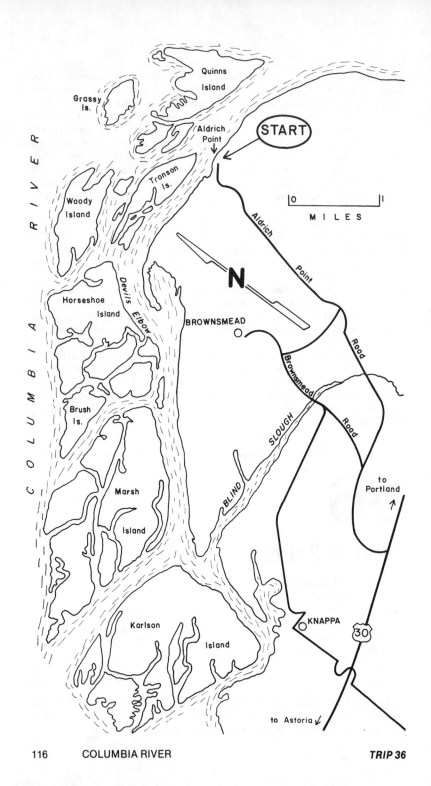

START

Quinns Island

Grassy Is.

Aldrich Point

COLUMBIA RIVER

Woody Island

Tronson Is.

N

0   1
M I L E S

Horseshoe Island

Devils Elbow

BROWNSMEAD

Aldrich Point Road

Brownsmead Road

Brush Is.

BLIND SLOUGH

to Portland

Marsh

Island

Karlson

Island

KNAPPA

30

to Astoria

Horseshoe Island

An excellent access point for visiting the eastern end of the refuge is Aldrich Point. From Portland, drive north and west on Highway 30. Eighteen miles past Clatskanie, look for a turnoff marked Brownsmead. Turn right, and follow the signs six miles to the boat ramp at Aldrich Point.

The main shipping channel on this part of the Columbia is close to the Washington shore. In contrast, the islands close to the Oregon side offer relatively undisturbed paddling. These islands all but disappear at high tide and are laced with mazes of passages and sloughs. Large grassy islands at low tide become mere marshes a few hours later, while narrow channels appear everywhere.

In the event of westerly winds, cross the channel immediately, and work your way west along Devils Elbow in the lee of Tronson and Horseshoe islands. The sloughs on these two islands alone will provide at least a full day's exploration. Carry a compass to help find your way out of their mazes, especially if fog threatens.

Remember, the tide can produce strong currents, even in the small channels, so don't paddle a long distance with the tide unless you are sure you have the time and strength to paddle back. Combined with the unpredictable wind, the tidal currents can make a short trip into a long one.

Contrary to popular belief, national wildlife refuges aren't exactly safe havens for birds. Only a small portion of the refuge is closed to hunters during the bird season. In the fall, call the refuge at (206) 795-4915 to determine if your trip is likely to be leadfilled. And at all times of the year, take your binoculars and bird book along. Spring and fall migrations provide opportunities to see dozens of species. In winter, two of the largest residents are the bald eagle and the whistling swan.

37

Cathlamet Bay

Location: 4 miles east of Astoria
Distance: variable
Time: 2 to 6 hours
USGS Maps: Astoria and Cathlamet 7.5′
NOAA Chart: #18531
Best Season: all year
Rating: A

If you want miles of open water with a marine atmosphere, but do not want to venture into the Pacific, try Cathlamet Bay in the Columbia River near Astoria.

Wait for a day with good weather, then drive north and west from Portland on Highway 30. One mile past the drawbridge over the John Day River, turn right at a public boat ramp. From Astoria, the ramp is 1.7 miles east of the Tongue Point turnoff; it is situated on the John Day River, a quarter mile from the bay.

From the ramp, turn left on the river and paddle under the railroad drawbridge. This bridge is manned 24 hours a day by a tender who lives in the house at the east end of the bridge.

The bay is large, and so are the islands. At high tide portions of these islands are flooded, and finding solid ground is not easy. Mott Island and Lois Island have dry areas, but Grassy Island is rather ethereal, since it is nonexistent at high tide. The north end of Lois Island has a sandy beach that would make a good lunch spot or campsite. Watch for deer.

If the weather is at all questionable, stay close to shore, or at least don't venture out beyond the protection of the islands and Tongue Point, which was named for its obvious shape by Capt. George Vancouver. Meriwether Lewis and William Clark tried to name it Point William, but the older more descriptive name stuck, so to speak. The point is now used as a Job Corps center and Coast Guard station.

If the wind picks up, or fog threatens, head for shore. Open water near the mouth of the Columbia is no place to be in bad weather. A foul-weather option would be to paddle up the John Day River, although it is only navigable for about 3.5 miles upstream from the boat ramp. The current on the river is mainly tidal.

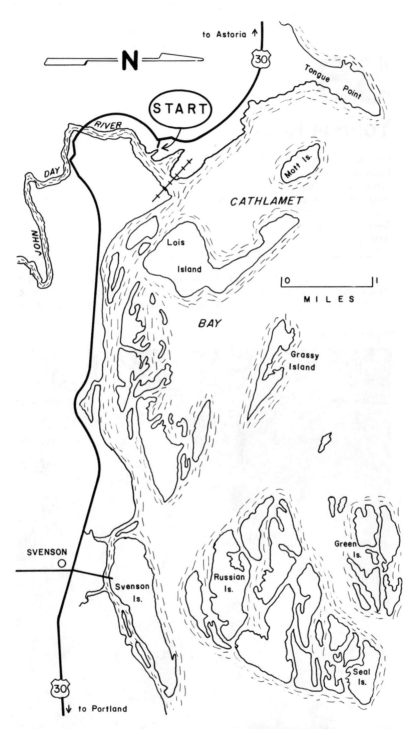

N

to Astoria ↑

30

Tongue Point

START

RIVER

DAY

JOHN

Mott Is.

CATHLAMET

Lois Island

0   1
M I L E S

BAY

Grassy Island

SVENSON ○

Svenson Is.

Green Is.

Russian Is.

30

↓ to Portland

Seal Is.

TRIP 37   COLUMBIA RIVER   119

38

Youngs River

Location: south of Astoria
Distance: 9 miles
Time: 4 to 5 hours
USGS Maps: Olney and Astoria 7.5′
NOAA Chart: #18521
Best Season: all year
Rating: A

Youngs River is a small but pretty stream that begins in the northern Coast Range and flows into the Columbia at Astoria. Described here is a nine-mile paddle from a bridge near Youngs River Falls to Astoria. The first part of the

Youngs River Falls

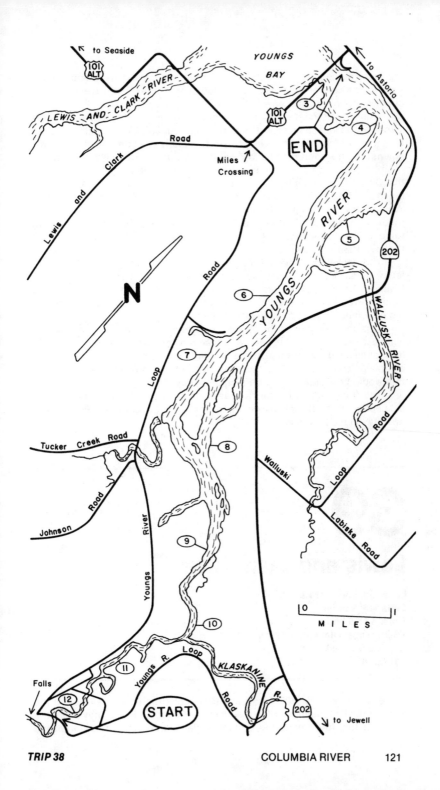

trip involves paddling on a small mountain stream, but as it approaches Astoria, the channel widens into a broad coastal river. The trip ends on the open waters of Youngs Bay.

This entire stretch of the river is influenced by the tide. If at all possible (especially in late summer and fall), try to plan your trip so that launching can be made at high tide. The benefits are twofold: you will not have to paddle against the tide, and the shallow water of the upper river will be navigable.

Start the trip by leaving an extra car at the public boat ramp located at the Clatsop Community College Maritime Science Center in Astoria. To reach the Center from downtown Astoria, drive south on Highway 101 to Youngs Bay. Turn east on Highway 101 Alternate (West Maritime Drive) and follow it to the north end of the Youngs Bay Bridge. The Center and boat ramp are located immediately east of the north end of the bridge. (See also the map from trip #39.)

Then drive south across the bridge. One mile south of the bridge turn left at Miles Crossing, and drive about seven miles to a bridge over Youngs River. (From the hairpin turn just west of the bridge, a short trail leads to Youngs River Falls.) If the water level at the bridge looks too low, try launching near mile 11 or 11.5; otherwise, launch at the bridge.

This upper section of the river is a delight on a hot day—cool and shady, with just enough current to keep your boat moving along. Eventually the river leaves the shady woods and starts winding its way through broad expanses of grassy islands and diked pastures. With little protection from the wind, this would be a slow paddle on a blustery day.

The final section of the river as it enters Youngs Bay is particularly susceptible to bad weather coming in from the Pacific Ocean. Play it safe, and stay close to shore.

39

Lewis and Clark River

Location: south of Astoria
Distance: 9 miles
Time: 4 to 5 hours
USGS Maps: Olney and Astoria 7.5′
Best Season: all year
Rating: A

In the winter of 1805-1806, Lewis and Clark constructed a small fort on the west bank of a stream near the mouth of the Columbia River. They spent the winter in this fort among the Clatsop Indians, who called the stream the

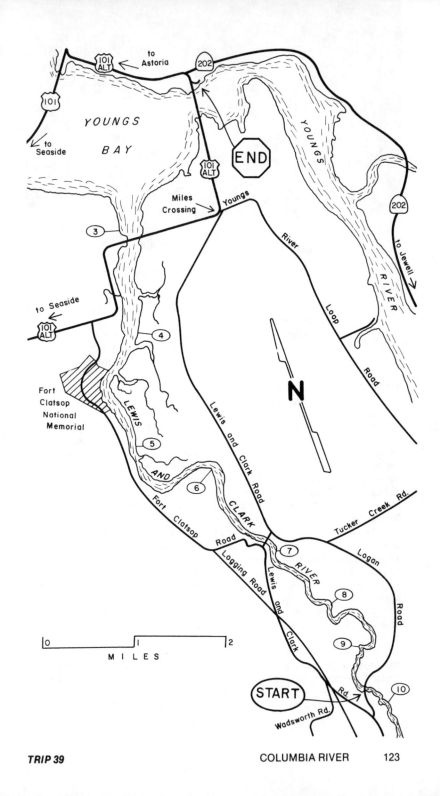

to Astoria

YOUNGS
BAY

to Seaside

Miles
Crossing

Youngs

END

YOUNGS RIVER

to Jewell

to Seaside

River

Loop

Road

N

Fort
Clatsop
National
Memorial

LEWIS

AND

CLARK

Lewis and Clark Road

Fort Clatsop Road

Logging Road

Tucker Creek Rd.

RIVER

Logan

Road

Lewis and Clark

START

Rd.

Wadsworth Rd.

0   1   2
M I L E S

Fort Clatsop

Netul River. Today, a replica of the fort has been built, and the river is named after its most famous visitors.

The lower 10 miles of the river are described here. Since this entire section is tidal and since the river is quite small, it is best to launch at high tide. If you disregard this advice, the upper part of the river may not be navigable, particularly late in the year. In addition, a low-tide launch will mean several hours of paddling against the tide. In fact, if a low-tide launch is planned, the canoeist will be better off paddling the trip in the direction opposite that described here.

For a high-tide launch, leave your extra car or bicycle at the public boat ramp near the north end of the Youngs Bay Bridge (U.S. 101 Alternate, not to be confused with the U.S. 101 bridge to the west). From downtown Astoria, the boat ramp is best reached by driving south on U.S. 101. Before U.S. 101 crosses Youngs Bay, turn east on U.S. 101 Alternate and Highway 202, and follow them about 1.25 miles to the Youngs Bay Bridge. Immediately east of the north end of the bridge is a small side road leading to a public boat ramp at the Clatsop Community College Maritime Science Center.

The launching point is reached by driving south on U.S. 101 Alternate across Young's Bay, then west across the mouth of the Lewis and Clark River. About a mile after crossing the river, turn left at a sign pointing to Fort Clatsop National Memorial. Follow the main road, staying on the west side of the river, about six miles to Logan Road. Turn left and park near the bridge.

The first few miles of the river are relatively wooded, but by mile 7 the scenery becomes predominantly pastoral. On a windy day, the pastures offer little protection.

At a broad bend in the river at mile 4.5, watch closely for an opening in the brush on the west bank, marking a canoe landing maintained by the National Park Service. (Occasionally, log rafts may limit access to the landing.) From the landing, a short trail leads to the replica of Fort Clatsop.

At mile 4, the river widens considerably as it begins to merge with Youngs Bay. Be wary of wind and waves when crossing the open waters of the bay.

40

Long Island

Location: near Long Beach, Washington
Distance: 2 to 15 miles
Time: 4 hours to overnight
USGS Map: Long Island 7.5′
NOAA Chart: #18504
Best Season: all year
Rating: A

Willapa Bay is one of the largest estuaries on the southern Washington coast. Its most prominent geographic features are the narrow Long Beach Peninsula, which forms the bay's western shore, and 5000-acre Long Island, which lies on the east side of the bay.

The bay and its shores are teeming with wildlife. Three sections of the estuary, including the southern end of the bay, Long Island, and the tip of the

Landing on Long Island

Camp on Long Island

peninsula, are part of the Willapa National Wildlife Refuge. Of the three areas, the island offers the best canoeing and wildlife observation. Its waters are relatively sheltered, and hunting is limited to bows and arrows. The island portion of the refuge is on Highway 101 about a dozen miles north of Ilwaco, Washington.

The bay has a unique history stretching back to Chinook Indian days. White men were first attracted by the logging opportunities, but they soon discovered that the oysters were equally abundant and valuable. Today, logging and oystering still thrive.

Despite establishment of the wildlife refuge, much of Long Island remains the property of lumber companies, although the federal government is expanding public ownership by trading trees for land. The best launch site to explore the island from is at the refuge headquarters, on Highway 101 near the southeast end of the island. A public boat ramp is located just across the highway from the headquarters.

Although much can be seen in a few hours, the size of the island and the activities available make a weekend trip more desirable. Camping is permitted at five campgrounds on the island, but drinking water must be carried from the mainland.

Shellfishing is probably the most popular activity. Clamming and crabbing are excellent, but the current oyster population has been planted and is considered private property.

The interior of the island can be explored by hiking the logging roads shown on the sketch map. An old-growth cedar grove is located near the south end of the island, daffodils cover parts of an old farm on High Point, and Diamond Point is maintained as a natural area. Throughout the island,

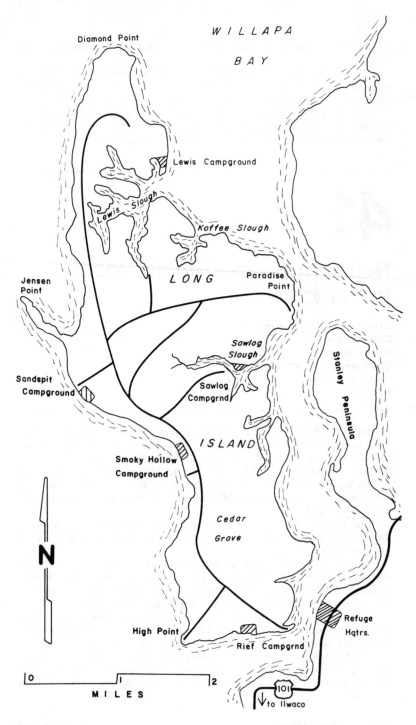

WILLAPA BAY

Diamond Point

Lewis Campground

Lewis Slough

Koffee Slough

Jensen Point

LONG

Paradise Point

Sawlog Slough

Sandspit Campground

Sawlog Campgrnd

Smoky Hollow Campground

ISLAND

Stanley Peninsula

Cedar Grove

N

High Point

Rief Campgrnd

Refuge Hqtrs.

0   1   2

MILES

101

↓ to Ilwaco

watch for black-tailed deer, Roosevelt elk, black bear, and countless bird species.

Be sure to take a tide table and a copy of the current NOAA chart with you. Since the tide can be very strong, time your travel to move with, not against it, and use the chart to find navigable water during low tide.

Another word of caution: Willapa Bay can be very rough in bad weather or when the tide is running. If the weather is at all questionable, stay close to shore, or, if necessary, wait on shore for storms to pass.

41

Nehalem River—Timber Road to Vernonia

Location: south of Vernonia
Distance: 9 miles
Time: 4 hours
USGS Maps: Birkenfeld and Vernonia 15'
Best Season: winter and early spring
Rating: C

The Nehalem River upstream from Vernonia is unique. In comparison with other canoeable streams in Oregon, it is tiny. In contrast with other parts of the Nehalem, it is navigable during only a fraction of the year. And due to the relatively steep drop of its channel, it is not for the inexperienced. If you are a neophyte paddler, but would like to paddle on the Nehalem, opt for one of the lower sections, particularly trip #44 (Roy Creek to Nehalem) or possibly #43 (Big Eddy to Mist).

The first requirement for this trip is the hardest to satisfy: wait for a tolerable day in winter or early spring. Then dig out your wool clothes, best rain gear, and driest boots.

From Highway 26 about 30 miles west of Portland, turn north on Highway 47 and drive to Vernonia. Turn right at the locomotive (Adams Street), and drive three blocks to Anderson Park. Leave an extra car or bicycle, and note the narrow private bridge that marks the end of the trip.

Then drive back towards Highway 26. About two miles south of Vernonia, turn right on unmarked Timber Road and follow it about five miles to the second bridge over the Nehalem. Launch under the bridge.

For the first few miles, the river passes through deep forests, with alders growing diagonally out over the water. Downstream the woods open up a bit, but alders, cedars, and firs, together with mosses and ferns, still dominate the scene.

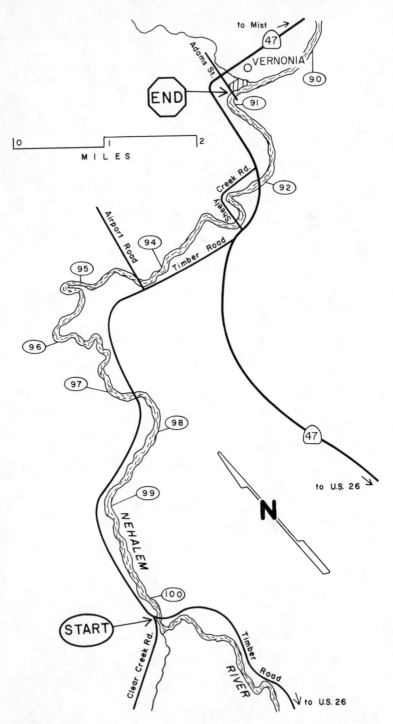

to Mist →

47

VERNONIA

90

Adams St.

END

91

92

Creek Rd.

Shelly

Airport Road

94

Timber Road

95

96

97

98

99

NEHALEM

47

to U.S. 26

N

100

START →

Clear Creek Rd.

Timber Road

RIVER

↓ to U.S. 26

0   1   2

MILES

You will encounter a few quiet pools, but most of your time will be spent watching the river play with your boat. Sharp curves, projecting logs, shallow rapids, and choices between two (or three) blind channels will provide little time for relaxation or lazy paddling.

Do not underestimate the strength of the current, or overestimate your ability to sneak through narrow curves. If you complete this section of the Nehalem without making several short portages across midriver gravel bars, you are either very skilled or quite fool-hardy (and very wet).

42

Nehalem River—Vernonia to Big Eddy

Location: north of Vernonia
Distance: 10 miles
Time: 4 to 5 hours
USGS Map: Vernonia 15′
Best Season: winter and early spring
Rating: C

The upper portions of the Nehalem River offer pleasant canoeing through a beautiful corner of the state. Deep forests, winding roads, and quaint small towns characterize the Columbia County region drained by this pretty river.

Once the site of an annual canoe race, the 10-mile stretch from Vernonia to Big Eddy County Park is a justifiably popular trip. Unlike most of the small flatwater streams in Oregon, the Nehalem has a strong clear current that drops fairly quickly through mountainous country. Do not paddle this trip unless you are fairly experienced at maneuvering your boat; the current is strong, and sharp turns are abundant.

The Nehalem is a shallow river, partly due to the geologic history of the area. If you glance at the banks of the river (particularly the west bank), you will notice that the river has cut its channel through shale, a sedimentary rock that tends to fracture horizontally, resulting in a relatively flat and broad riverbed. Due to the shallow channel, this trip should be done only in winter or early spring. After about April, your boat will suffer from a journey on this section of the Nehalem. To do the trip, leave an extra car or bicycle at Big Eddy County Park, 8.5 miles north of Vernonia on Highway 47 towards Mist. Highway 47 can be reached by driving west from Portland on Highway 26 about 30 miles.

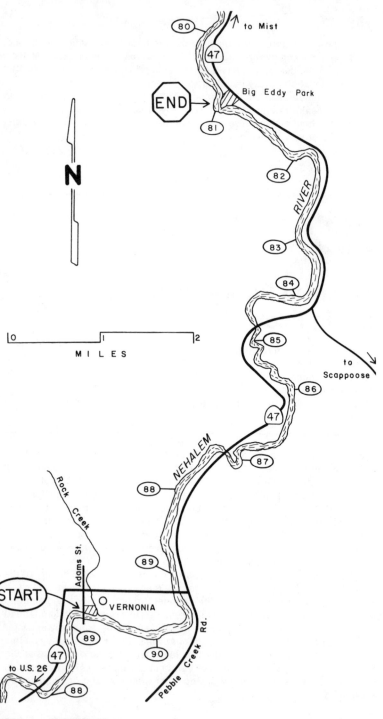

This trip is particularly well suited for using a bicycle as the transportation to fetch your car at the end of the trip. The pedal from Big Eddy back to Vernonia is short, flat, and scenic.

The launching point is Anderson Park at the foot of Adams Street in Vernonia. As you drive through Vernonia, turn south at the locomotive and drive about three blocks to the park. (The park north of the locomotive is the wrong park, since it is on Rock Creek.) In Anderson Park, the best launching site is near the private bridge.

Do not dismiss Vernonia as just another logging town. It is a quiet, slow-paced community far enough from the major highways to have retained its character. Stop long enough to visit the Columbia County Historical Society Museum and to admire the beautiful brick elementary school (particularly in contrast to the "modern" high school).

This trip is marked by several bridges. The first one, about a mile after launching, has a sharp drop beneath it. Be careful.

After this bridge, the road to Mist parallels the river. The road is often quite close, but the traffic is light and rarely spoils the journey.

The paved boat ramp at Big Eddy will appear suddenly on the right as you make a sharp right turn. Keep an eye open for it, unless you plan on visiting Mist, nine miles downstream.

43

Nehalem River—Big Eddy to Mist

Location: north of Vernonia
Distance: 9 miles
Time: 3 to 5 hours
USGS Maps: Vernonia and Birkenfeld 15′
Best Season: winter through late spring
Rating: C

The tiny town of Mist was not named for its size, but it is easily missed. The town was actually named for its damp weather. No matter what time of year you visit, there is sure to be some fog hanging over the pastures and forests that surround Mist.

The paddle from Big Eddy Park to Mist is smooth and calm compared to sections of the river upstream (trips #41 and #42). The current, however, can be quite strong, even though the topographic maps show that the river drops very little in the nine-mile stretch. In winter, the paddle might take less than three hours, but by midspring the river slows a bit, making for a more leisurely trip.

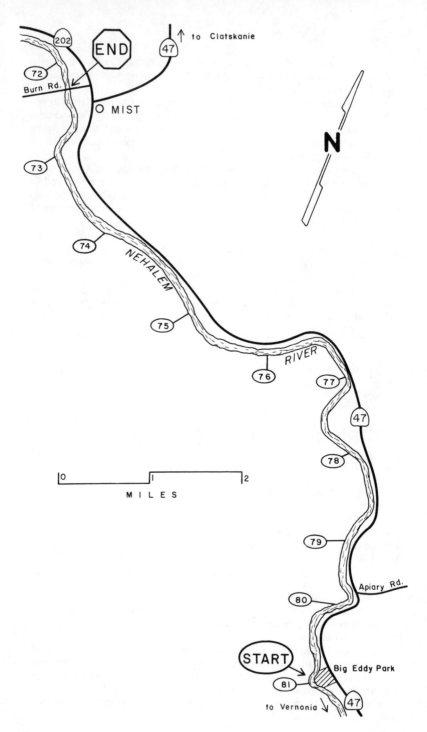

202

END

72

Burn Rd.

47 ↑ to Clatskanie

O MIST

N

73

74

NEHALEM

75

RIVER

76

77

47

78

0   1   2

MILES

79

Apiary Rd.

80

START   Big Eddy Park

81

to Vernonia ↓   47

Unlike its upstream counterparts, this section of the Nehalem is navigable until late spring most years. In case of doubt, the river can be checked easily, since Highway 47 follows it closely.

The trip is started by leaving an extra car (or bicycle) near Mist. To reach Mist, drive west from Portland about 30 miles on Highway 26. Turn north on Highway 47 and follow it through Vernonia to Mist. A block west of town on Highway 202, turn south on Burn Road and drive one block to Vivian's Bridge. Park your vehicle near the bridge.

Then return to Mist, and drive south on Highway 47 about nine miles to the county park at Big Eddy. After entering the park, drive straight ahead to the boat ramp at the far side of the park.

Although Highway 47 is often just a few feet from the river's north bank and much of the forest south of the river has been clear cut, this stretch of the river is still quite scenic. Beautiful alders line both banks and dangle long streamers of moss toward the water. Belted kingfishers dart from side to side in search of small fish, and frogs croak from their hiding places on the damp banks.

For the most part, the water is perfectly flat, but a few spots require some care. Keep your eyes downstream for logs or other debris, which you must skirt on one side or the other, and in a few other places for brief stretches of choppy water.

At Vivian's Bridge, the best landing spot is just upstream from its north end. Do not paddle downstream from the bridge unless you have carefully examined the rapids not far below.

P.S. On your way home, do not neglect to stop at the Mist General Store, a Columbia County fixture since 1874.

44

Nehalem River—Roy Creek to Nehalem

Location: Nehalem
Distance: 6.5 miles
Time: 3 to 4 hours
USGS Maps: Nehalem 15′
Best Season: all year
Rating: A

The Nehalem River valley carves a huge crescent across the northwest corner of Oregon. From its source in northwestern Washington County, it flows north through Columbia County, then west through Clatsop County to the

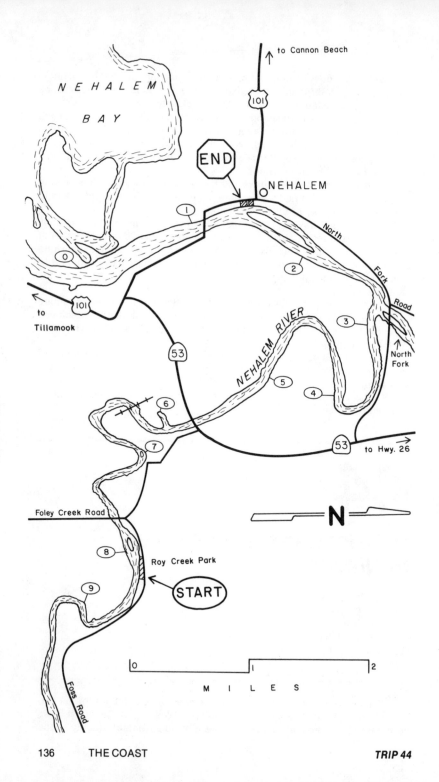

NEHALEM BAY

to Cannon Beach

101

END

NEHALEM

①

North

⓪

Fork

to
Tillamook

101

53

Road

③

North
Fork

NEHALEM RIVER

⑤

②

④

⑥

53

to Hwy. 26

⑦

N

Foley Creek Road

⑧

Roy Creek Park

⑨

START

0   1   2

M I L E S

Foss Road

river's mouth in Tillamook County, a total distance of more than a hundred miles.

The short paddle described here covers 6.5 miles of the river from Roy Creek Park, where the river first becomes tidal, to the town of Nehalem. Check the tide tables before you launch; if you do not want to be paddling against the tide, or if you want to be sure of sufficiently deep water late in the year, try to start paddling close to high tide, or shortly thereafter.

The trip begins by leaving an extra car or bicycle at either of the two public docks on Highway 101 in Nehalem. Then drive south on Highway 101 and cross the river to the junction with Highway 53, where you should turn left. A mile later, just after another bridge over the Nehalem, turn right on Foss Road and drive a half mile to Roy Creek Park.

Although the park is many miles upstream from the Pacific, the water level is affected by the tide. At low tide, particularly in late summer or fall, be careful of shallow spots. At mile 7, a shallow area among several islands is best passed on the extreme right.

Despite possible shallow water, a fall trip on this river is particularly pleasant. Fall colors line the route, along with dozens of fishermen. Once the author and companions spent several minutes watching a fisherman play a huge steelhead until being told that he had been at it for more than two hours. Farther downstream, a red-tailed hawk sat on the top of a Douglas fir, perhaps hoping for a similar opportunity.

Fisherman's shack on the lower Nehalem River

Wildlife along the lower Nehalem River

These miles of the Nehalem are hardly pristine wilderness, but the fishermen, the dairy farms, and the small cottages along the banks create a serene, pastoral atmosphere. The last half mile takes paddlers behind a large island that lies just off the town of Nehalem.

45

Tillamook Bay

Location: near Tillamook
Distance: variable
Time: 4 to 5 hours
USGS Maps: Nehalem and Tillamook 15'
NOAA Chart: #18558
Best Season: all year
Rating: A

Tillamook Bay is one of the largest on the Oregon Coast. The Tillamook, Trask, Wilson, Kilchis, and Miami rivers all empty into this 6 × 3 mile bay,

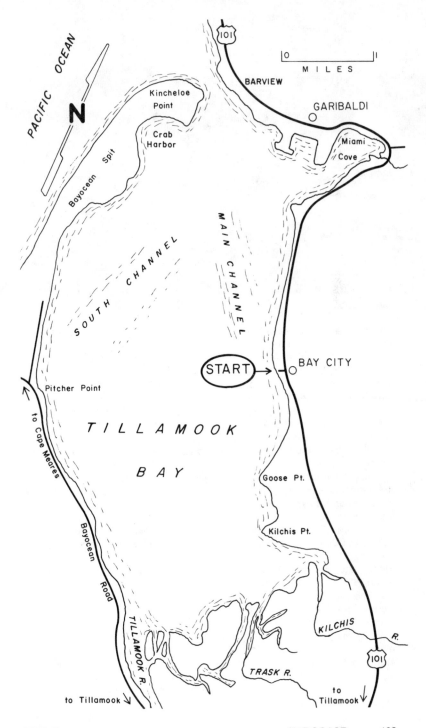

PACIFIC OCEAN

N

101

BARVIEW

GARIBALDI

MILES
0   1

Miami
Cove

Kincheloe
Point

Crab
Harbor

Bayocean Spit

MAIN CHANNEL

SOUTH CHANNEL

START → ○ BAY CITY

Pitcher Point

to Cape Meares

Bayocean Road

TILLAMOOK

BAY

Goose Pt.

Kilchis Pt.

KILCHIS R.

TILLAMOOK R.

TRASK R.

101

to Tillamook →

to
Tillamook ↓

Tillamook Bay

which is the home of several small towns. The bay is also noted for its large and diverse bird population.

The most interesting feature of the bay is the huge spit which forms its western side. Shortly after the turn of the century, a large resort community named Bayocean was developed on this spit, which was then an island. A ferry from Garibaldi was used to reach the community of 1600 lots centered around a hotel and natatorium. A causeway eventually connected the island to Pitcher Point. Erosion problems plagued the community until a 1948 storm broke through the island in several places. The town was eventually abandoned. Unfortunately, modern developers have yet to learn Bayocean's lesson.

Several launching sites are available. A road leads part of the way out the Bayocean causeway, but due to large mud flats, launching from it requires a careful eye on the tides and a close scrutiny of a current chart to locate water deep enough to float a canoe.

A more reliable launching site is the Bay City municipal landing on Highway 101 at Bay City. Be cautious of the effects of tidal currents throughout this bay. Use them to your advantage, but be aware of the possibility of rough water, particularly when the currents cross shallow areas. Avoid the mouth of the bay at all times.

The Bayocean spit makes an excellent lunch spot, especially at Crab Harbor where landing is relatively easy. Hike across the spit for views of the ocean; also watch for deer.

No matter what time of year you visit Tillamook Bay, take your binoculars and bird book along. Fall and winter birdwatching ensures outstanding sightings, including hawks, owls, falcons, loons, bald eagles, and egrets, plus numerous species of gulls and ducks. Throughout the year the most obvious birds include great blue herons and cormorants. In the summer, brown pelicans can be seen diving for fish.

46

Nestucca River

Location: Pacific City
Distance: 9 miles
Time: 4 hours
USGS Map: Hebo 15′
Best Season: late fall through spring
Rating: B

The Nestucca River is a beautiful clear stream that drains the Coast Range south of Tillamook. It is a very small river; only the lowest portion is navigable most of the year. The trip described here passes through several picturesque coastal towns; it starts near Hebo, paddles past Cloverdale and Woods, and ends in Pacific City.

   Start the trip by leaving an extra car or bicycle at the public boat ramp just south of Pacific City. From the center of the town, the ramp is reached by driving west on Pacific Avenue. After crossing the bridge over the river, turn south on Sunset Drive and watch for a left turn marked by a boat ramp

Cloverdale

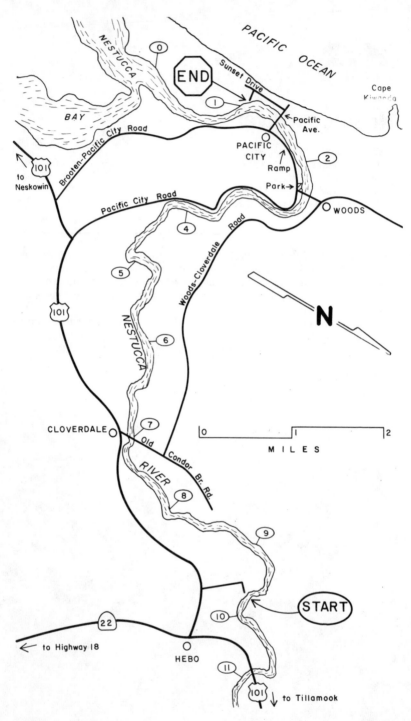

PACIFIC OCEAN

NESTUCCA

BAY

Cape Kiwanda

⓪

END

Sunset Drive

①

Pacific Ave.

Brooten-Pacific City Road

to 101 Neskowin

PACIFIC CITY

Ramp

②

Park→

Pacific City Road

④

WOODS

⑤

Woods-Cloverdale Road

101

NESTUCCA

⑥

N

0   1   2
MILES

CLOVERDALE

⑦

Old Condor Br. Rd.

RIVER

⑧

⑨

START

22

⑩

to Highway 18

HEBO

⑪

101

to Tillamook

sign. (For a slightly shorter trip, a public boat ramp is also located on the east side of the river about 0.2 miles north of the bridge.)

The launching point is west of the town of Hebo. From Pacific City, drive north and east on Pacific City Road to Highway 101, and follow it 4.4 miles east to a left turn marked by a boat ramp sign. Follow this road to its end.

Most of this section of the Nestucca River is tidal, so a launch at high tide is preferable, but not essential.

The first mile or two of the river drops fairly rapidly and has a strong current to it, but the river quickly reaches tidewater and winds its leisurely way to the sea. The channel makes a few quick turns in this first section, but any pair who has learned the basic canoe strokes should get through unscathed.

After paddling a few miles, you will not need this guidebook to tell you that the lower Nestucca Valley is dairy country. Something in the air will let you know.

The valley is broad and flat, although occasionally the river channel nudges up against the steep hills that define it. Since the valley is close to the ocean and quite wide, it is subject to moderately strong winds. Although the trip is a short one, you might check the weather forecast before launching. Paddling into a headwind has only one reward: if you are using a bicycle to return to your car, the return trip will be relatively effortless.

Siletz River—Siletz to Morgan Park

Location: northeast of Newport
Distance: 12 miles
Time: 3 to 4 hours
USGS Maps: Toledo and Euchre Mountain 15′
Best Season: spring
Rating: C

If you are looking for a river with more excitement than the usual flatwater trip, this could be the one for you. Although this 12-mile section of the Siletz River is not known for tight corners or difficult maneuvering, it can offer rougher water than any of the other trips described in this book.

Paddling this trip may whet your appetite to venture into more difficult whitewater situations; or then again, it may get you just plain wet. Since the hardest parts of this trip are in the first half, you might consider launching midway, at Ojalla Bridge, if you are not sure you are ready for the rough water upstream. Even so, the lower half has plenty of swift water to deal with.

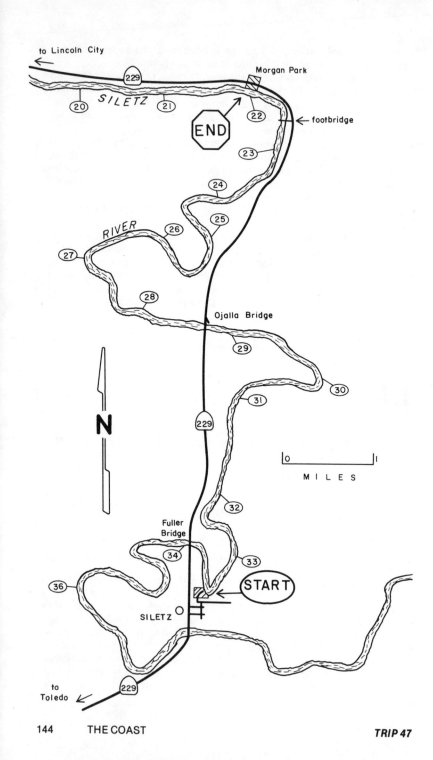

to Lincoln City

229

SILETZ

20   21

Morgan Park

22

← footbridge

END

23

24

25

RIVER

26

27

28

Ojalla Bridge

29

30

31

229

N

0   1

MILES

32

Fuller
Bridge

34   33

START

36

SILETZ

to
Toledo

229

On the Siletz River

Start the trip by leaving an extra car or bicycle at Morgan County Park on Highway 229. From Lincoln City, the park can be reached by driving south on Highway 101 to the Siletz River bridge, then turning east on Highway 229 and driving 18 miles. The park can be reached from the south, by driving east from Newport on Highway 20 to Toledo, then turning north on Highway 229.

While at Morgan Park, take a good look at the surroundings, since the park is extremely difficult to recognize from the river until after it has been passed. Note the parking lot/clearing and the small island just off the boat ramp.

The launching point for the complete trip is Old Mill Park in Siletz, six miles south of Morgan Park on Highway 229. In Siletz, drive one block east on Metcalf Street, then one block north on Kobielski Street; turn left on Mill Park Drive.

For those wanting a bit less excitement, a primitive boat landing is available at Ojalla Bridge, three miles north of Siletz. The landing is on the east side of the bridge's north end.

Due to the strong current, these are fast trips. The portion above Ojalla Bridge takes only an hour when the water is high, and the lower part can sometimes be paddled in an hour and a half.

The roughest rapids are a short distance downstream from Old Mill Park. After turning the first bend, the rapids begin on both sides of a small island. Landing at the head of the island to scout the rapids may be a good idea, but be careful of the strong current. In 1981, the left channel seemed to be the best choice. Small rapids occur throughout the trip, although they steadily diminish in size and frequency.

Morgan Park, 0.7 miles below a suspension footbridge, will be difficult to spot from the river, since the area is quite brushy and the boat ramp is well concealed. Keep your eyes open for a clearing in the trees (the parking lot), and try to land at the base of a trail a few feet upstream from the boat ramp.

On the Siletz River

48

Siletz River—Morgan Park
to Strome Park

Location: south of Lincoln City
Distance: 8 miles
Time: 4 hours
USGS Maps: Euchre Mountain and Cape Foulweather 15′
Best Season: winter through early summer
Rating: B

The Siletz River is a long, undulating coastal stream that drains much of northern Lincoln County. Unusual for its aimless course, the river is constantly twisting and turning in every possible direction.

The section described here involves such a twist. The river travels west for five miles, then makes a lazy U-turn and returns in an easterly direction for two miles. Paddling this section has one distinct advantage for those who use a bicycle to return to the launching point from the end of the trip, since the distance by road is only four miles.

To start this trip, drive north from Depoe Bay, or south from Lincoln City, on Highway 101 to Siletz Bay. Just north of the bridge over the Siletz River,

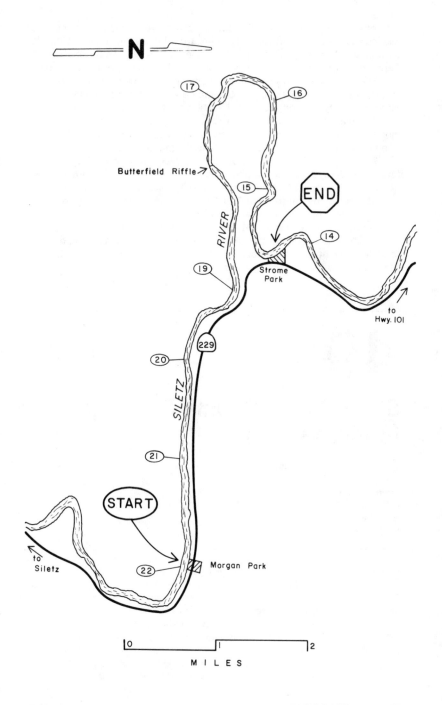

N

Butterfield Riffle

RIVER

END

Strome
Park

to
Hwy. 101

SILETZ

229

START

to
Siletz

Morgan Park

0   1   2
M I L E S

TRIP 48   THE COAST   147

turn east on Highway 229 and follow it up the river. Almost 14 miles after leaving Highway 101, and about 3.5 miles after the pavement ends, watch for an unmarked gravel road on the right, leading downhill to Strome County Park. Leave your extra car or bicycle near the boat ramp at this small park.

Then continue driving east on Highway 229. The pavement resumes shortly. About four miles east of Strome Park, watch for signs designating Morgan County Park on the right. Launch your boat from the boat ramp.

At times, launching from this ramp can be a little tricky, due to the moderately strong current and some brush just downstream from the ramp. It is not difficult, but be prepared to fend off the bushes.

This section of the Siletz is particularly pleasant on a hot day, as it offers many shady portions and placid pools of cool water. A few gravelly sections, however, may become quite shallow by midsummer.

At mile 18, the "Butterfield Riffle" is shown on most maps. The riffle apparently only exists at low water. Since this portion of the river is influenced by the tide, you may or may not encounter these small rapids.

Landmarks are rare in this area of the river. A compass should be used to determine approximate location from time to time, particularly near Strome Park, which is easy to miss.

49

Siletz River—Strome Park to Pikes Camp

Location: south of Lincoln City
Distance: 12 miles
Time: 7 hours
USGS Map: Euchre Mountain 15′
Best Season: all year
Rating: B

In this 12-mile section, the Siletz River changes from a small mountain stream to a broad tidal river. The upper portion of the trip involves paddling on a shady stream with a fairly strong current, while the lower portion is wide and slow, with only the current generated by the tide.

This is a long trip for a single day of paddling, especially if the wind and tide are both moving in from the ocean. Plan the outing for a day when the tide will be on its way out during much of your trip. Another option would be to paddle only a portion of the section described here. Although there are no public boat ramps between Strome Park and Pikes Camp, several commer-

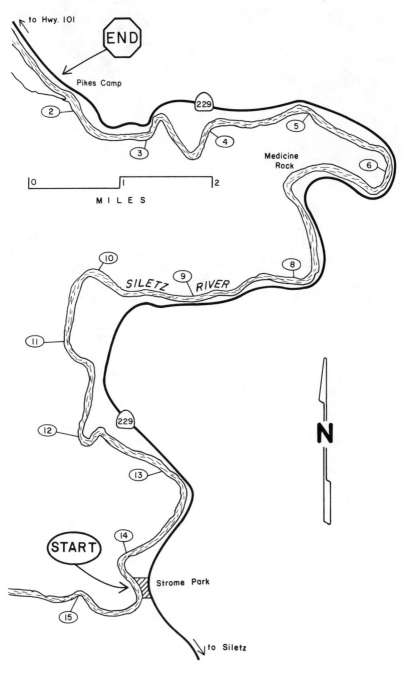

Siletz River near Pikes Camp

cial marinas along the route permit boat launching for a small fee. The marinas are all located along Highway 229; you can pick one the day of your trip, or plan ahead by getting a copy of *A Guide to Oregon Boating Facilities* from the State Marine Board (see introduction).

The trip begins by driving north from Depoe Bay, or south from Lincoln City, on Highway 101 to the intersection with Highway 229, just north of the Siletz River bridge. Turn east on Highway 229 and follow it 1.4 miles to an area known as Pikes Camp. The area is best recognized by the house just across the river, which was used in the filming of the movie version of the Ken Kesey novel *Sometimes a Great Notion*. Leave your extra car on the shoulder, then continue east 12.5 miles to an unmarked gravel road on the right, which leads downhill to Strome County Park with its primitive boat ramp.

If the tide is out, the first part of the trip will involve a moderately strong current. Late in the year, you may encounter a few shallow spots, another reason for launching at high tide.

At mile 7, watch for a large rock slab exposed on the hillside a few feet from the left riverbank. This is Medicine Rock, believed in Siletz Indian lore to be the home of an evil medicine man. It was the Indians' custom to leave offerings at the base of the rock to appease the evil spirit.

The last half of this trip involves steady paddling on a long stretch of flat water.

50

Yaquina River

Location: east of Newport
Distance: 10.5 miles
Time: 5 to 6 hours
USGS Map: Toledo 15′
Best Season: all year
Rating: A

The Yaquina River flows into the Pacific Ocean just south of Newport. Its huge bay is noted for its oyster population. As one drives east up the Ya-

Covered bridge at Elk City

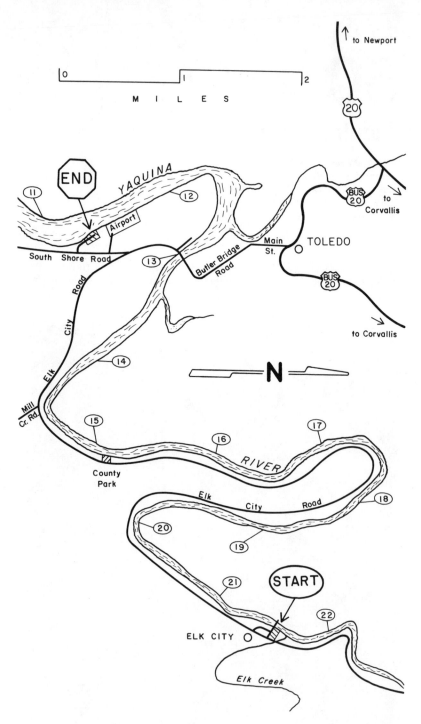

Elk City store

quina Valley, the first town encountered is Toledo, with its lumber and pulp mills.

Three miles, as the crow flies, east of Toledo lies a cluster of about a dozen buildings known as Elk City. The town's largest structure is a covered bridge that was built in 1922. Although the bridge was closed in 1980, patrons of the Elk City Store have been informed that the bridge will be rehabilitated in the near future.

This trip paddles the 10.5-mile distance from this forgotten hamlet to its modern industrial neighbor, Toledo. The tide reaches all the way to Elk City, so the paddler can expect little or no aid from the current. This is a fairly long trip for a pair of novices, especially if the wind and tide are not cooperating. A county boat ramp about halfway between the two towns would be a good ending point for those desiring a shorter trip. (The upper half of this trip is the more scenic of the two.)

To paddle this trip, drive east from Newport on Highway 20, and follow Highway 20 Business into Toledo. Turn right on Main Streeet and follow it as it becomes Butler Bridge Road. Following the signs to the airport, cross the bridge and take the second right turn. Just past the airport, turn right to a public boat ramp where you can leave your extra car.

Return to Butler Bridge Road (now Elk City Road), turn right, and follow it to Elk City. Although the road eventually becomes gravel, it is in good condition. In Elk City, a public park and boat ramp are just upstream from the covered bridge.

As is obvious from the sketch map, the river channel is a unique series of undulations of increasing size. Paddlers should have little difficulty determining their location on this section of the Yaquina. Since most of the travel is either due north or due south, just remember how many U-turns have been made.

A sand bar along the Lewis River

INDEX